The Essential Poet

*BOOK/CASSETTE PACKAGES AVAILABLE

The Essential Robinson

Edwin Arlington Robinson
BORN 22 DECEMBER 1869
DIED 6 APRIL 1935

The Essential
ROBINSON

Selected and with an
Introduction by

DONALD HALL

The Ecco Press

Introduction and selection copyright © 1994 by Donald Hall

All rights reserved
The Ecco Press
100 West Broad Street, Hopewell, NJ 08525
Published simultaneously in Canada by
Penguin Books Canada Ltd., Ontario
Printed in the United States of America
Designed by Reg Perry
FIRST EDITION

Library of Congress Cataloging-in-Publication Data

Robinson, Edwin Arlington, 1869–1935.
The essential Robinson / selected and with an introduction by
Donald Hall.
p. cm. -- (The Essential poets ; vol. 19)
I. Hall, Donald, 1928- .   II. Title.   III. Series: Essential
poets (New York, N.Y.) ; v. 19.
PS3535.025A6   1993
811'.52--dc20   *93-14493*
ISBN 0-88001-336-2

Portrait of Edwin Arlington Robinson from a painting by Lilla Cabot Perry.

Contents

❖❖

The Essential Robinson

Introduction

❖

In 1869, Edwin Arlington Robinson was born in the village of Head Tide in Maine, third son and final child of Edward and Mary Robinson; his brothers Dean and Herman were twelve and four. Because his mother had wanted a daughter, Robinson began life as a disappointment; he went unnamed for half a year. When a summer visitor insisted that the six-month-old baby be named, "Edwin" was chosen by lot; the poet's middle name remembered the provenance of the visitor. As he grew up in Gardiner, where the family moved shortly after his birth, this poet of failure and defeat was known as "Win"; he preferred "Long Robinson" himself—at six-foot-two, he was tall for his generation—but his friends later settled for "E.A.R.," which was appropriate enough: The near-anonymity of initials fitted the shadowy silence of his character; and he had a beautiful ear.

Perhaps because she never welcomed him, Robinson doted on his mother. His father prospered while the Union did—storekeeper, small-time banker, investor—and favored his second son, Herman, businessman and entrepreneur. Robinson loathed Herman (not coincidentally, he adored Herman's wife, Emma) while he admired his elder brother, Dean, who became a doctor. Then the family fell apart in a rapid series of disasters: Dean became addicted to morphine; the 1893 panic destroyed Herman's fortunes and Edward's investments in Herman's schemes; Edward took to drink and died; not much later, Mary died of diphtheria. Remnants of the Robinson fortune bought a Gardiner drugstore, at least partly as a source for Dean's mor-

| 3 |

phine. Then Dean died, probably by deliberate overdose, and Herman turned alcoholic, hawking lobsters in Gardiner's streets while Emma took in sewing. Later, Herman died in the public ward of a Massachusetts hospital.

E.A.R. never took a college degree; but to graduate from a good high school in the 1890s was to know history and languages. He made close friends at Harvard, where he spent two years as a special student, and where he first published in undergraduate magazines. He studied philosophy, English literature, and languages—without distinguishing himself—but Harvard was his entry into a larger world, his release from provincialism; he indulged himself happily in bibulous Cambridge talk. Robinson loved cities; all his life, he doted on theater, opera, and orchestral music.

By his midtwenties the character had emerged that endured until death. E.A.R. refused with few exceptions to hold down a job or work for a living. He was "a confirmed bachelor," as the cliché has it, with a calling for solitude; the phrase was not a euphemism for homosexuality. Like other males of his time, Robinson presumably sought professional relief when he was young— he wrote poems about prostitutes—but his erotic experience was probably limited. A frequently repeated story has him rejecting an offer from Isadora Duncan. Some of his friends in their reminiscences hint at love affairs; certainly he cherished unacceptable love for his brother's wife and widow. It is clear that several times in his life he thought about marriage, especially to the beautiful Emma after Herman's death; but we may doubt that he came close.

E.A.R. was affectionate, as his letters show, but in person he was shy and often dumb. Many anecdotes illustrate his silence, or immense silences terminated by monosyllables. Only late at night, after considerable whiskey, did Robinson become voluble; if he was alcoholic at times, like his father and brother, surely drink was self-medication for shyness, silence, and melancholy. When he finally found readers, when summers at the MacDowell Colony added structure and society to his year, he stopped drinking—only to resume later in response to the Volstead Act, which he considered "fundamentally evil and arbitrary."

When he was not married to whiskey, he was married to art. If he read Yeats's poem about choosing perfection of the life or of the work, he never doubted the choice. He wrote in a letter, "Do you know I have a theory that Browning's life-long happiness with his wife is all humbug? The man's life was in his art." Maybe his concentration on the art of poetry compensated for love's loss: his mother's; Emma's. Whatever its irrational source, his devotion to making poetry remained fundamental. All his life, he characterized himself as someone who could do only one thing.

In Gardiner after high school, before and after his brief stint at Harvard, he lived at home as a sort of servant or hired man, tending the garden and doing odd jobs, working at his poetry as he could. After his mother died he moved to fin de siècle New York. For twenty years he survived on a tiny inheritance, on the charity of others, and on free lunches in saloons; he turned down the journalistic opportunities that largely supported rival poets. He labored for a while as timekeeper for workers constructing the subway. Back in Massachusetts, he failed as an office boy at Harvard. Returning to New York, he continued the old Bohemian life of furnished rooms and patched clothing. "I starved twenty years," he said late in life, "and in my opinion no one should write poetry unless he is willing to starve for it." Once he laboriously accumulated nickels toward a new pair of trousers, then plunged his savings into a Metropolitan Opera ticket for *Tristan und Isolde*. Continually he worked at his verses, sitting in a rocking chair in a bare room high over a New York street, solitary and industrious, revising his lines over and over again. On several occasions he worked on stories and plays, trying to earn a living with his pen, but failed utterly. He was right, however much he fulfilled his own prophecy: Poetry was the one thing he could do.

Which made it a pity that no one thought he could do it.

E.A.R. published his first book at his own expense in 1896. He mailed out many copies, receiving letters of praise but no significant attention. His second and third books—many essential poems derive from the early volumes—appeared because of subsidies or guarantees from more affluent friends. Magazine editors rejected his best work, at a time when many magazines printed what passed for poems, because they were realistic. (Although Robinson admired Zola, remember that he wrote at a time when *Jude* was obscene.) In the 1890s and the 1900s, poems told cheerful lies in words considered pretty: As Robinson bragged of his first book (1896), "there is not a red-bellied robin in the whole collection." It was daring, shocking, and unacceptable to write sonnets about butchers overcome with grief or about hired men who spoke the common language. After a decade of assiduous labor and continual discouragement, Robinson sank into alcoholic depression. "For seven years," he told a friend late in his life, over a tumbler of whiskey, "I had *ab-so-lute-ly* nothing but the bottle." His friend reports that E.A.R. loved to say *"ab-so-lute-ly."*

Then, early in the century, before the Great War, several things happened almost at once. The first event was most astonishing—a letter with a White House frank. Theodore Roosevelt's son Kermit attended Groton, where an English master from Gardiner, Maine, showed him the unknown poet's poems; impressed, Kermit showed his father in the White House—who was dazzled, and who found Robinson in New York and offered to help: Would the poet take a consular position in Mexico or Canada? Robinson settled for a sinecure in customs in New York—he loved New York—which allowed him to help Herman's widow and daughters when they needed it. T.R. then bullied his own publisher into reissuing a Robinson volume and reviewed Robinson's poems from the presidential desk; of course, opposition newspapers ridiculed the incumbent's taste.

Two further miracles were required. First was the MacDowell Colony in Peterborough, New Hampshire—just beginning—which E.A.R. visited reluctantly and was amazed to enjoy. MacDowell provided a structure for the remainder of his structureless life; every summer from 1911 on E.A.R. rocking-chaired in a MacDowell studio. He visited Massachusetts friends in spring and fall, and spent his winters in New York, but Peterborough was the frame for his year's house. For most colonists, MacDowell is a release from family life into creative solitude; for E.A.R. the colony *was* family life. He sat in his own chair for dinner, indulging his "idiom of silence," as a friend called it, among a knot of artists year after year.

The third miracle was the gradual emergence of an American literary and artistic culture or community, of which MacDowell itself was a sign. America had already produced great artists, but some had lived much of the time in Europe; some had been learned and provincial in Massachusetts (Emerson, Longfellow, Thoreau, Hawthorne); and some had been the magnificent eccentrics (Whitman, Dickinson, Melville) who were our greatest writers—masters or mistresses of separation, who lived at the brilliant margin of the national life.

Then, in 1912, Harriet Monroe started *Poetry* in Chicago (poetry in *Chicago*!) and Ezra Pound, corresponding from London, supplied her with T. S. Eliot, H. D. Imagiste—and Robert Frost. Pound, Eliot, and H.D. still required Europe, but now *Poetry* (also: *Broom; Secession; The Dial; Others; The Little Review;* and also: the Armory Show; Stieglitz) and its ambiance rendered the United States possible for poets who worked in a community, like most artists over history. Wallace Stevens, Marianne Moore, and William Carlos Williams did not need to carry their sensibilities to England or France or Italy. Instead, they argued about linebreaks and Marcel Duchamp at weekend picnics in New Jersey.

When E.A.R. finally turned famous, the monthlies that had rejected him for decades started to court him (the way the *Atlantic*, played like a fiddle by Robert Frost, printed Frost poems that they had earlier rejected). E.A.R.'s personal tide turned beginning when he was fifty: prizes, honorary degrees, and money (*Tristram* sold almost sixty thousand copies its first year). The old Bohemian, with indecent speed, became a figure of respectable eminence. It is seldom observed that E.A.R. also published in *Poetry*—with Eliot's "Love Song of J. Alfred Prufrock," with Pound and Stevens and Moore. In one issue—March 1914—Harriet Monroe published Carl Sandburg's most famous poem, "Chicago" ("Hog butcher to the world," etc.), and the poem "Eros Turannos," which is arguably Robinson's best.

"Eros Turannos" tells about a marriage, in a Maine coastal town, between a fortune hunter and a woman of old family who marries to avoid solitary old age. Robinson catches the man's opportunism and the woman's desperation.

> *She fears him, and will always ask*
>   *What fated her to choose him;*
> *She meets in his engaging mask*
>   *All reasons to refuse him;*
> *But what she meets and what she fears*
> *Are less than are the downward years,*
> *Drawn slowly to the foamless weirs*
>   *Of age, were she to lose him.*
>
> *A sense of ocean and old trees*
>   *Envelops and allures him;*

> *Tradition, touching all he sees,*
> > *Beguiles and reassures him;*
> *And all her doubts of what he says*
> *Are dimmed with what she knows of days—*
> *Till even prejudice delays*
> > *And fades, and she secures him.*

It does not take long before she understands her error; she se-
cludes herself while townspeople gossip about her eccentricity or
madness:

> *The falling leaf inaugurates*
> > *The reign of her confusion;*
> *The pounding wave reverberates*
> > *The dirge of her illusion;*
> *And home, where passion lived and died,*
> *Becomes a place where she can hide,*
> *While all the town and harbor side*
> > *Vibrate with her seclusion.*

There follows a stanza of padding and needless qualification. Such
wasted motion often annoys us in Robinson; we learn to scan such
passages quickly, bored but anticipatory, to reach his constructed
conclusion:

> *Meanwhile we do no harm; for they*
> > *That with a god have striven,*
> *Not hearing much of what we say,*
> > *Take what the god has given;*
> *Though like waves breaking it may be,*
> *Or like a changed familiar tree,*
> *Or like a stairway to the sea*
> > *Where down the blind are driven.*

The first four lines reaffirm the title: Her struggle, not with a secular king but with a divine tyrant, achieves nothing but madness and dysphoria.

Robinson tells his story in a stanza form that might seem fitted to light verse. (Yvor Winters noted that Robinson's prosody borrows from W. M. Praed's.) He constructs his stanza out of a quatrain made of tetrameters and trimeters, the B-rhymes double, followed by a tetrameter tercet and concluded by a trimeter, the last line double-rhyming with lines two and four. How can such a jingle render feeling?

Here's how: His similes are structural, not decorative, as "like waves breaking" embodies the relentless dolor of a featureless daily life; as "like a changed familiar tree" puns on "family tree" and combines ancestral pride with debasement; as "like a stairway to the sea" foreshadows inevitable descent into death, recalls the "foamless weirs / Of age," and suggests possible suicide by drowning—tyrannical Love driving its victim into the sea. These similes conclude the poem with a passage that is tragic, ironic—and gorgeous.

But it cannot be ironic in its metrical form—or gorgeous in its compressed and witty style—unless the reader's ear is conditioned by the glorious tradition of meter in English: another reason for the diminishment of this poet's reputation.

Although he wrote creditable book-length poems in blank verse, the best of Robinson's poems are rhymed and brief. In this short book, I represent his blank verse by poems of moderate length: "Isaac and Archibald" is best, a wonderful poem in blank verse derived (like Frost's) from Wordsworth; slightly less valuable is "Rembrandt to Rembrandt." For glories in a more Tennysonian blank verse, look at the lush conclusions to *Merlin* and *Tristram*.

A few fine lyrics describe the natural world, existing for their own sweet sakes, for the joy or ecstasy of their saying or singing:

Dark hills at evening in the west,
Where sunset hovers like a sound
Of golden horns that sang to rest
Old bones of warriors under ground,
Far now from all the bannered ways
Where flash the legions of the sun,
You fade—as if the last of days
Were fading, and all wars were done.

"The Dark Hills" compares landscape to romance, and Robinson is more moved by Roman legionaries or King Arthur than by Mount Monadnock.

Usually, by Heraclitean paradox, the man of silence and solitude wrote poems about people, poems of character and story. His narrative sonnets provide a characteristic signature: usually a bizarre or extraordinary story. A prostitute's sonnet ("The Growth of 'Lorraine'") ends: "'I'm going to the devil.'—And she went." We read of a dying blind man ("Ben Trovato") whose mistress has fled, whose wife wears the mistress's fur so that he will die mistaken (and content) over whose hand he holds. Again and again we read of suicide ("The Mill") and failure, of business as greed and ruin, of capitulation to twin devils of drugs and alcohol. Or we read of the butcher's grief:

Reuben Bright

Because he was a butcher and thereby
Did earn an honest living (and did right),
I would not have you think that Reuben Bright
Was any more a brute than you or I;
For when they told him that his wife must die,
He stared at them, and shook with grief and fright,
And cried like a great baby half that night,
And made the women cry to see him cry.

And after she was dead, and he had paid
The singers and the sexton and the rest,
He packed a lot of things that she had made
Most mournfully away in an old chest
Of hers, and put some chopped-up cedar boughs
In with them, and tore down the slaughter house.

Robinson's octave ends with wild grief; but the active imagination of the sestet is his genius—the cow-killer converted. This sonnet's beauty is not diminished by the great proof hack in its initial printing, where the last phrase ran: ". . . tore down to the slaughter house."

For other narratives of character read *passim,* not forgetting early work ("Luke Havergal," from the Harvard years, captivated T.R.) in this chronological selection. Few of his philosophical poems succeed: "The Man against the Sky" and "Octaves" do not think so well; an exception is "Hillcrest," dour and fierce, relentlessly intelligent:

Who sees unchastened here the soul
Triumphant has no other sight
Than has a child who sees the whole
World radiant with his own delight.

Far journeys and hard wandering
Await him in whose crude surmise
Peace, like a mask, hides everything
That is and has been from his eyes;

And all his wisdom is unfound,
Or like a web that error weaves
On airy looms that have a sound
No louder now than falling leaves.

The best work remains anecdotal and ethical, like "The Poor Re-lation," "Isaac and Archibald," "Eros Turannos," and—why not?—"Mr. Flood's Party," which is funny and miserable with an appropriate misery. With a subject—loneliness in old age—suggesting sentimentality, Robinson mocks himself and his old man by an overreaching reference to Roland's horn, and by a triple-switch that goes the necessary step beyond expectation: He sets us up with a sentimental simile—

> *Then, as a mother lays her sleeping child*
> *Down tenderly, fearing it may awake,*

and then swoops the chair from beneath our descendant back-sides—

> *He set the jug down slowly at his feet*
> *With trembling care,*

so that, with a gross vaudeville humor, we laugh at the joke—his baby is the jug!—until Robinson takes genius's third step:

> *knowing that most things break.*

This lesson Robinson knew from his family and Gardiner, Maine.

If we are old enough, we grew up learning that modern poetry *has* to be difficult; therefore, "Mr. Flood's Party" cannot be modern poetry, or maybe (by idiotic extension) poetry at all. According to this requirement, neither Frost nor Hardy can be poets either—and indeed I remember the 1940s, when the poems of Frost and Hardy were inadmissible or at least embarrassing and awkward of admission. By the end of this century, we have brought Hardy and Frost back without (let me hope) needing to expel Eliot, Ste-vens, Moore, Williams, and Pound.

We must bring Robinson back. Although he remains among the best American poets, Robinson now goes largely unread. An insidious form of neglect enshrines one minor effort, genuflects, and bypasses the best work. Robinson is remembered chiefly for a brief story in quatrains, punchy as a television ad, in which the protagonist surprises us (once) by putting a bullet through his head.

Robinson was the poet chosen by lot as sacrifice to modernism. The poetic enemy, addressed at the turn of the century by the young T. S. Eliot and Ezra Pound, was someone like Richard Watson Gilder—not Robinson—but by the 1930s no one knew Gilder's name; and Robinson was momentarily notorious for multiple Pulitzers and for writing a best-selling blank-verse Arthurian narrative. When he was young, Robinson sounded like no one else—and paid the price; but to the unhistoric ear of a later era, Robinson's poetry, when set beside "The Waste Land," sounded Victorian. If the combative Eliot needed to dismiss Robinson as "negligible," it is understandable. But surely we need no longer dismiss the author of "Eros Turannos" and "Isaac and Archibald" because he wrote iambics in a coherent syntax.

We must restore Robinson to the American pantheon. The generation of great poets, after the magnificent solitaries Dickinson and Whitman, begins with Robinson and Frost before it moves to Pound, Stevens, Moore, and Eliot. Robinson was essential to this motion, in his realism or honesty, and in his relentless care for the art of poetic language. Reading his letters or his sparse table talk, one encounters his dour, unforgiving professionalism. Woe to the friend who counts "fire" as two syllables or who heaps one preposition on top of another.

Robinson was master of verse and poetry, of metric and diction, syntax and tone, rhyme and understanding, ethics, metaphor, and the exposure of greed. The last nouns in this series are not disconnected from the first: Dead metaphors are unethical, and forced rhymes are corrupt. In monkish solitude, with painstaking and moral attention, in long hours of revision, he made great poems. Once at MacDowell, at an evening meal, he was outraged to hear someone boast of having written hundreds of lines that day. Speaking slowly, or stingily, he told how he had spent four hours in the morning placing a hyphen between two words—and four hours in the afternoon taking it out.

DONALD HALL

Poems

John Evereldown

"Where are you going to-night, to-night,—
    Where are you going, John Evereldown?
There's never the sign of a star in sight,
    Nor a lamp that's nearer than Tilbury Town.
Why do you stare as a dead man might?
Where are you pointing away from the light?
And where are you going to-night, to-night,—
    Where are you going, John Evereldown?"

"Right through the forest, where none can see,
    There's where I'm going, to Tilbury Town.
The men are asleep,—or awake, may be,—
    But the women are calling John Evereldown.
Ever and ever they call for me,
And while they call can a man be free?
So right through the forest, where none can see,
    There's where I'm going, to Tilbury Town."

"But why are you going so late, so late,—
    Why are you going, John Evereldown?
Though the road be smooth and the way be straight,
    There are two long leagues to Tilbury Town.
Come in by the fire, old man, and wait!

Why do you chatter out there by the gate?
And why are you going so late, so late,—
        Why are you going, John Evereldown?"

"I follow the women wherever they call,—
        That's why I'm going to Tilbury Town.
God knows if I pray to be done with it all,
        But God is no friend to John Evereldown.
So the clouds may come and the rain may fall,
The shadows may creep and the dead men crawl,—
But I follow the women wherever they call,
        And that's why I'm going to Tilbury Town."

Luke Havergal

Go to the western gate, Luke Havergal,
There where the vines cling crimson on the wall,
And in the twilight wait for what will come.
The leaves will whisper there of her, and some,
Like flying words, will strike you as they fall;
But go, and if you listen she will call.
Go to the western gate, Luke Havergal—
Luke Havergal.

No, there is not a dawn in eastern skies
To rift the fiery night that's in your eyes;
But there, where western glooms are gathering,
The dark will end the dark, if anything:
God slays Himself with every leaf that flies,
And hell is more than half of paradise.
No, there is not a dawn in eastern skies—
In eastern skies.

Out of a grave I come to tell you this,
Out of a grave I come to quench the kiss
That flames upon your forehead with a glow
That blinds you to the way that you must go.
Yes, there is yet one way to where she is,
Bitter, but one that faith may never miss.
Out of a grave I come to tell you this—
To tell you this.

There is the western gate, Luke Havergal,
There are the crimson leaves upon the wall.
Go, for the winds are tearing them away,—
Nor think to riddle the dead words they say,
Nor any more to feel them as they fall;
But go, and if you trust her she will call.
There is the western gate, Luke Havergal—
Luke Havergal.

The House on the Hill

They are all gone away,
    The House is shut and still,
There is nothing more to say.

Through broken walls and gray
    The winds blow bleak and shrill:
They are all gone away.

Nor is there one to-day
    To speak them good or ill:
There is nothing more to say.

Why is it then we stray
        Around the sunken sill?
They are all gone away,

And our poor fancy-play
        For them is wasted skill:
There is nothing more to say.

There is ruin and decay
        In the House on the Hill:
They are all gone away,
There is nothing more to say.

Richard Cory

Whenever Richard Cory went down town,
We people on the pavement looked at him:
He was a gentleman from sole to crown,
Clean favored, and imperially slim.

And he was always quietly arrayed,
And he was always human when he talked;
But still he fluttered pulses when he said,
"Good-morning," and he glittered when he walked.

And he was rich—yes, richer than a king—
And admirably schooled in every grace:
In fine, we thought that he was everything
To make us wish that we were in his place.

So on we worked, and waited for the light,
And went without the meat, and cursed the bread;
And Richard Cory, one calm summer night,
Went home and put a bullet through his head.

Dear Friends

Dear friends, reproach me not for what I do,
Nor counsel me, nor pity me; nor say
That I am wearing half my life away
For bubble-work that only fools pursue.
And if my bubbles be too small for you,
Blow bigger then your own: the games we play
To fill the frittered minutes of a day,
Good glasses are to read the spirit through.

And whoso reads may get him some shrewd skill;
And some unprofitable scorn resign,
To praise the very thing that he deplores;
So, friends (dear friends), remember, if you will,
The shame I win for singing is all mine,
The gold I miss for dreaming is all yours.

The Story of the Ashes and the Flame

No matter why, nor whence, nor when she came,
There was her place. No matter what men said,
No matter what she was; living or dead,
Faithful or not, he loved her all the same.
The story was as old as human shame,

But ever since that lonely night she fled,
With books to blind him, he had only read
The story of the ashes and the flame.

There she was always coming pretty soon
To fool him back, with penitent scared eyes
That had in them the laughter of the moon
For baffled lovers, and to make him think—
Before she gave him time enough to wink—
Her kisses were the keys to Paradise.

Amaryllis

Once, when I wandered in the woods alone,
An old man tottered up to me and said,
"Come, friend, and see the grave that I have made
For Amaryllis." There was in the tone
Of his complaint such quaver and such moan
That I took pity on him and obeyed,
And long stood looking where his hands had laid
An ancient woman, shrunk to skin and bone.

Far out beyond the forest I could hear
The calling of loud progress, and the bold
Incessant scream of commerce ringing clear;
But though the trumpets of the world were glad,
It made me lonely and it made me sad
To think that Amaryllis had grown old.

Zola

Because he puts the compromising chart
Of hell before your eyes, you are afraid;
Because he counts the price that you have paid
For innocence, and counts it from the start,
You loathe him. But he sees the human heart
Of God meanwhile, and in His hand was weighed
Your squeamish and emasculate crusade
Against the grim dominion of his art.

Never until we conquer the uncouth
Connivings of our shamed indifference
(We call it Christian faith) are we to scan
The racked and shrieking hideousness of Truth
To find, in hate's polluted self-defence
Throbbing, the pulse, the divine heart of man.

The Pity of the Leaves

Vengeful across the cold November moors,
Loud with ancestral shame there came the bleak
Sad wind that shrieked, and answered with a shriek,
Reverberant through lonely corridors.
The old man heard it; and he heard, perforce,
Words out of lips that were no more to speak—
Words of the past that shook the old man's cheek
Like dead, remembered footsteps on old floors.

And then there were the leaves that plagued him so!
The brown, thin leaves that on the stones outside
Skipped with a freezing whisper. Now and then

They stopped, and stayed there—just to let him know
How dead they were, but if the old man cried,
They fluttered off like withered souls of men.

Aaron Stark

Withal a meagre man was Aaron Stark,
Cursed and unkempt, shrewd, shrivelled, and morose.
A miser was he, with a miser's nose,
And eyes like little dollars in the dark.
His thin, pinched mouth was nothing but a mark;
And when he spoke there came like sullen blows
Through scattered fangs a few snarled words and close,
As if a cur were chary of its bark.

Glad for the murmur of his hard renown,
Year after year he shambled through the town,
A loveless exile moving with a staff;
And oftentimes there crept into his ears
A sound of alien pity, touched with tears,—
And then (and only then) did Aaron laugh.

Cliff Klingenhagen

Cliff Klingenhagen had me in to dine
With him one day; and after soup and meat,
And all the other things there were to eat,
Cliff took two glasses and filled one with wine
And one with wormwood. Then, without a sign
For me to choose at all, he took the draught
Of bitterness himself, and lightly quaffed
It off, and said the other one was mine.

And when I asked him what the deuce he meant
By doing that, he only looked at me
And smiled, and said it was a way of his.
And though I know the fellow, I have spent
Long time a-wondering when I shall be
As happy as Cliff Klingenhagen is.

The Clerks

I did not think that I should find them there
When I came back again; but there they stood,
As in the days they dreamed of when young blood
Was in their cheeks and women called them fair.
Be sure, they met me with an ancient air,—
And yes, there was a shop-worn brotherhood
About them; but the men were just as good,
And just as human as they ever were.

And you that ache so much to be sublime,
And you that feed yourselves with your descent,
What comes of all your visions and your fears?
Poets and kings are but the clerks of Time,
Tiering the same dull webs of discontent,
Clipping the same sad alnage of the years.

Fleming Helphenstine

At first I thought there was a superfine
Persuasion in his face; but the free glow
That filled it when he stopped and cried, "Hollo!"
Shone joyously, and so I let it shine.
He said his name was Fleming Helphenstine,

But be that as it may;—I only know
He talked of this and that and So-and-So,
And laughed and chaffed like any friend of mine.

But soon, with a queer, quick frown, he looked at me,
And I looked hard at him; and there we gazed
In a strained way that made us cringe and wince:
Then, with a wordless clogged apology
That sounded half confused and half amazed,
He dodged,—and I have never seen him since.

Reuben Bright

Because he was a butcher and thereby
Did earn an honest living (and did right),
I would not have you think that Reuben Bright
Was any more a brute than you or I;
For when they told him that his wife must die,
He stared at them, and shook with grief and fright,
And cried like a great baby half that night,
And made the women cry to see him cry.

And after she was dead, and he had paid
The singers and the sexton and the rest,
He packed a lot of things that she had made
Most mournfully away in an old chest
Of hers, and put some chopped-up cedar boughs
In with them, and tore down the slaughter house.

The Tavern

Whenever I go by there nowadays
And look at the rank weeds and the strange grass,
The torn blue curtains and the broken glass,
I seem to be afraid of the old place;
And something stiffens up and down my face,
For all the world as if I saw the ghost
Of old Ham Amory, the murdered host,
With his dead eyes turned on me all aglaze.

The Tavern has a story, but no man
Can tell us what it is. We only know
That once long after midnight, years ago,
A stranger galloped up from Tilbury Town,
Who brushed, and scared, and all but overran
That skirt-crazed reprobate, John Evereldown.

George Crabbe

Give him the darkest inch your shelf allows,
Hide him in lonely garrets, if you will,—
But his hard, human pulse is throbbing still
With the sure strength that fearless truth endows.
In spite of all fine science disavows,
Of his plain excellence and stubborn skill
There yet remains what fashion cannot kill,
Though years have thinned the laurel from his brows.

Whether or not we read him, we can feel
From time to time the vigor of his name
Against us like a finger for the shame

And emptiness of what our souls reveal
In books that are as altars where we kneel
To consecrate the flicker, not the flame.

Verlaine

Why do you dig like long-clawed scavengers
To touch the covered corpse of him that fled
The uplands for the fens, and rioted
Like a sick satyr with doom's worshippers?
Come! let the grass grow there; and leave his verse
To tell the story of the life he led.
Let the man go: let the dead flesh be dead,
And let the worms be its biographers.

Song sloughs away the sin to find redress
In art's complete remembrance: nothing clings
For long but laurel to the stricken brow
That felt the Muse's finger; nothing less
Than hell's fulfilment of the end of things
Can blot the star that shines on Paris now.

Supremacy

There is a drear and lonely tract of hell
From all the common gloom removed afar:
A flat, sad land it is, where shadows are,
Whose lorn estate my verse may never tell.
I walked among them and I knew them well:
Men I had slandered on life's little star
For churls and sluggards; and I knew the scar
Upon their brows of woe ineffable.

But as I went majestic on my way,
Into the dark they vanished, one by one,
Till, with a shaft of God's eternal day,
The dream of all my glory was undone,—
And, with a fool's importunate dismay,
I heard the dead men singing in the sun.

The Clinging Vine

"Be calm? And was I frantic?
    You'll have me laughing soon.
I'm calm as this Atlantic,
    And quiet as the moon;
I may have spoken faster
    Than once, in other days;
For I've no more a master,
    And now—'Be calm,' he says.

"Fear not, fear no commotion,—
    I'll be as rocks and sand;
The moon and stars and ocean
    Will envy my command;
No creature could be stiller
    In any kind of place
Than I . . . No, I'll not kill her;
    Her death is in her face.

"Be happy while she has it,
    For she'll not have it long;
A year, and then you'll pass it,
    Preparing a new song.
And I'm a fool for prating

Of what a year may bring,
When more like her are waiting
For more like you to sing.

"You mock me with denial,
You mean to call me hard?
You see no room for trial
When all my doors are barred?
You say, and you'd say dying,
That I dream what I know;
And sighing, and denying,
You'd hold my hand and go.

"You scowl—and I don't wonder;
I spoke too fast again;
But you'll forgive one blunder,
For you are like most men:
You are,—or so you've told me,
So many mortal times,
That heaven ought not to hold me
Accountable for crimes.

"Be calm? Was I unpleasant?
Then I'll be more discreet,
And grant you, for the present,
The balm of my defeat:
What she, with all her striving,
Could not have brought about,
You've done. Your own contriving
Has put the last light out.

"If she were the whole story,
If worse were not behind,
I'd creep with you to glory,

Believing I was blind;
I'd creep, and go on seeming
    To be what I despise.
You laugh, and say I'm dreaming,
    And all your laughs are lies.

"Are women mad? A few are,
    And if it's true you say—
If most men are as you are—
    We'll all be mad some day.
Be calm—and let me finish;
    There's more for you to know.
I'll talk while you diminish,
    And listen while you grow.

"There was a man who married
    Because he couldn't see;
And all his days he carried
    The mark of his degree.
But you—you came clear-sighted,
    And found truth in my eyes;
And all my wrongs you've righted
    With lies, and lies, and lies.

"You've killed the last assurance
    That once would have me strive
To rouse an old endurance
    That is no more alive.
It makes two people chilly
    To say what we have said,
But you—you'll not be silly
    And wrangle for the dead.

"You don't? You never wrangle?
          Why scold then,—or complain?
More words will only mangle
          What you've already slain.
Your pride you can't surrender?
          My name—for that you fear?
Since when were men so tender,
          And honor so severe?

"No more—I'll never bear it.
          I'm going. I'm like ice.
My burden? You would share it?
          Forbid the sacrifice!
Forget so quaint a notion,
          And let no more be told;
For moon and stars and ocean
          And you and I are cold."

Cassandra

I heard one who said: "Verily,
          What word have I for children here?
Your Dollar is your only Word,
          The wrath of it your only fear.

"You build it altars tall enough
          To make you see, but you are blind;
You cannot leave it long enough
          To look before you or behind.

"When Reason beckons you to pause,
     You laugh and say that you know best;
But what it is you know, you keep
     As dark as ingots in a chest.

"You laugh and answer, 'We are young;
     O leave us now, and let us grow.'—
Not asking how much more of this
     Will Time endure or Fate bestow.

"Because a few complacent years
     Have made your peril of your pride,
Think you that you are to go on
     Forever pampered and untried?

"What lost eclipse of history,
     What bivouac of the marching stars,
Has given the sign for you to see
     Millenniums and last great wars?

"What unrecorded overthrow
     Of all the world has ever known,
Or ever been, has made itself
     So plain to you, and you alone?

"Your Dollar, Dove and Eagle make
     A Trinity that even you
Rate higher than you rate yourselves;
     It pays, it flatters, and it's new.

"And though your very flesh and blood
     Be what your Eagle eats and drinks,
You'll praise him for the best of birds,
     Not knowing what the Eagle thinks.

"The power is yours, but not the sight;
    You see not upon what you tread;
You have the ages for your guide,
    But not the wisdom to be led.

"Think you to tread forever down
    The merciless old verities?
And are you never to have eyes
    To see the world for what it is?

"Are you to pay for what you have
    With all you are?"—No other word
We caught, but with a laughing crowd
    Moved on. None heeded, and few heard.

Stafford's Cabin

Once there was a cabin here, and once there was a man;
And something happened here before my memory began.
Time has made the two of them the fuel of one flame
And all we have of them is now a legend and a name.

All I have to say is what an old man said to me,
And that would seem to be as much as there will ever be.
"Fifty years ago it was we found it where it sat."—
And forty years ago it was old Archibald said that

"An apple tree that's yet alive saw something, I suppose,
Of what it was that happened there, and what no mortal
    knows.
Some one on the mountain heard far off a master shriek,
And then there was a light that showed the way for men to
    seek.

"We found it in the morning with an iron bar behind,
And there were chains around it; but no search could ever
        find,
Either in the ashes that were left, or anywhere,
A sign to tell of who or what had been with Stafford there.

"Stafford was a likely man with ideas of his own—
Though I could never like the kind that likes to live alone;
And when you met, you found his eyes were always on your
        shoes,
As if they did the talking when he asked you for the news.

"That's all, my son. Were I to talk for half a hundred years
I'd never clear away from there the cloud that never clears.
We buried what was left of it,—the bar, too, and the chains;
And only for the apple tree there's nothing that remains."

Forty years ago it was I heard the old man say,
"That's all, my son."—And here again I find the place to-day,
Deserted and told only by the tree that knows the most,
And overgrown with golden-rod as if there were no ghost.

Hillcrest

(TO MRS. EDWARD MACDOWELL)

No sound of any storm that shakes
Old island walls with older seas
Comes here where now September makes
An island in a sea of trees.

Between the sunlight and the shade
A man may learn till he forgets
The roaring of a world remade,
And all his ruins and regrets;

And if he still remembers here
Poor fights he may have won or lost,—
If he be ridden with the fear
Of what some other fight may cost,—

If, eager to confuse too soon,
What he has known with what may be,
He reads a planet out of tune
For cause of his jarred harmony,—

If here he venture to unroll
His index of adagios,
And he be given to console
Humanity with what he knows,—

He may by contemplation learn
A little more than what he knew,
And even see great oaks return
To acorns out of which they grew.

He may, if he but listen well,
Through twilight and the silence here,
Be told what there are none may tell
To vanity's impatient ear;

And he may never dare again
Say what awaits him, or be sure
What sunlit labyrinth of pain
He may not enter and endure.

Who knows to-day from yesterday
May learn to count no thing too strange:
Love builds of what Time takes away,
Till Death itself is less than Change.

Who sees enough in his duress
May go as far as dreams have gone;
Who sees a little may do less
Than many who are blind have done;

Who sees unchastened here the soul
Triumphant has no other sight
Than has a child who sees the whole
World radiant with his own delight.

Far journeys and hard wandering
Await him in whose crude surmise
Peace, like a mask, hides everything
That is and has been from his eyes;

And all his wisdom is unfound,
Or like a web that error weaves
On airy looms that have a sound
No louder now than falling leaves.

Eros Turannos

She fears him, and will always ask
    What fated her to choose him;
She meets in his engaging mask
    All reasons to refuse him;
But what she meets and what she fears

Are less than are the downward years,
Drawn slowly to the foamless weirs
    Of age, were she to lose him.

Between a blurred sagacity
    That once had power to sound him,
And Love, that will not let him be
    The Judas that she found him,
Her pride assuages her almost,
As if it were alone the cost.—
He sees that he will not be lost,
    And waits and looks around him.

A sense of ocean and old trees
    Envelops and allures him;
Tradition, touching all he sees,
    Beguiles and reassures him;
And all her doubts of what he says
Are dimmed with what she knows of days—
Till even prejudice delays
    And fades, and she secures him.

The falling leaf inaugurates
    The reign of her confusion;
The pounding wave reverberates
    The dirge of her illusion;
And home, where passion lived and died,
Becomes a place where she can hide,
While all the town and harbor side
    Vibrate with her seclusion.

We tell you, tapping on our brows,
    The story as it should be,—
As if the story of a house

Were told, or ever could be;
We'll have no kindly veil between
Her visions and those we have seen,—
As if we guessed what hers have been,
    Or what they are or would be.

Meanwhile we do no harm; for they
    That with a god have striven,
Not hearing much of what we say,
    Take what the god has given;
Though like waves breaking it may be,
Or like a changed familiar tree,
Or like a stairway to the sea
    Where down the blind are driven.

The Unforgiven

When he, who is the unforgiven,
Beheld her first, he found her fair:
No promise ever dreamt in heaven
Could then have lured him anywhere
That would have been away from there;
And all his wits had lightly striven,
Foiled with her voice, and eyes, and hair.

There's nothing in the saints and sages
To meet the shafts her glances had,
Or such as hers have had for ages
To blind a man till he be glad,
And humble him till he be mad.
The story would have many pages,
And would be neither good nor bad.

And, having followed, you would find him
Where properly the play begins;
But look for no red light behind him—
No fumes of many-colored sins,
Fanned high by screaming violins.
God knows what good it was to blind him,
Or whether man or woman wins.

And by the same eternal token,
Who knows just how it will all end?—
This drama of hard words unspoken,
This fireside farce, without a friend
Or enemy to comprehend
What augurs when two lives are broken,
And fear finds nothing left to mend.

He stares in vain for what awaits him,
And sees in Love a coin to toss;
He smiles, and her cold hush berates him
Beneath his hard half of the cross;
They wonder why it ever was;
And she, the unforgiving, hates him
More for her lack than for her loss.

He feeds with pride his indecision,
And shrinks from what will not occur,
Bequeathing with infirm derision
His ashes to the days that were,
Before she made him prisoner;
And labors to retrieve the vision
That he must once have had of her.

He waits, and there awaits an ending,
And he knows neither what nor when;
But no magicians are attending
To make him see as he saw then,
And he will never find again
The face that once had been the rending
Of all his purpose among men.

He blames her not, nor does he chide her,
And she has nothing new to say;
If he were Bluebeard he could hide her,
But that's not written in the play,
And there will be no change to-day;
Although, to the serene outsider,
There still would seem to be a way.

Veteran Sirens

The ghost of Ninon would be sorry now
To laugh at them, were she to see them here,
So brave and so alert for learning how
To fence with reason for another year.

Age offers a far comelier diadem
Than theirs; but anguish has no eye for grace,
When time's malicious mercy cautions them
To think a while of number and of space.

The burning hope, the worn expectancy,
The martyred humor, and the maimed allure,
Cry out for time to end his levity,
And age to soften its investiture;

But they, though others fade and are still fair,
Defy their fairness and are unsubdued;
Although they suffer, they may not forswear
The patient ardor of the unpursued.

Poor flesh, to fight the calendar so long;
Poor vanity, so quaint and yet so brave;
Poor folly, so deceived and yet so strong,
So far from Ninon and so near the grave.

Another Dark Lady

Think not, because I wonder where you fled,
That I would lift a pin to see you there;
You may, for me, be prowling anywhere,
So long as you show not your little head:
No dark and evil story of the dead
Would leave you less pernicious or less fair—
Not even Lilith, with her famous hair;
And Lilith was the devil, I have read.

I cannot hate you, for I loved you then.
The woods were golden then. There was a road
Through beeches; and I said their smooth feet showed
Like yours. Truth must have heard me from afar,
For I shall never have to learn again
That yours are cloven as no beech's are.

The Voice of Age

She'd look upon us, if she could,
As hard as Rhadamanthus would;
Yet one may see,—who sees her face,
Her crown of silver and of lace,
Her mystical serene address
Of age alloyed with loveliness,—
That she would not annihilate
The frailest of things animate.

She has opinions of our ways,
And if we're not all mad, she says,—
If our ways are not wholly worse
Than others, for not being hers,—
There might somehow be found a few
Less insane things for us to do,
And we might have a little heed
Of what Belshazzar couldn't read.

She feels, with all our furniture,
Room yet for something more secure
Than our self-kindled aureoles
To guide our poor forgotten souls;
But when we have explained that grace
Dwells now in doing for the race,
She nods—as if she were relieved;
Almost as if she were deceived.

She frowns at much of what she hears,
And shakes her head, and has her fears;
Though none may know, by any chance,
What rose-leaf ashes of romance
Are faintly stirred by later days

That would be well enough, she says,
If only people were more wise,
And grown-up children used their eyes.

The Dark House

Where a faint light shines alone,
Dwells a Demon I have known.
Most of you had better say
"The Dark House," and go your way.
Do not wonder if I stay.

For I know the Demon's eyes,
And their lure that never dies.
Banish all your fond alarms,
For I know the foiling charms
Of her eyes and of her arms,

And I know that in one room
Burns a lamp as in a tomb;
And I see the shadow glide,
Back and forth, of one denied
Power to find himself outside.

There he is who is my friend,
Damned, he fancies, to the end—
Vanquished, ever since a door
Closed, he thought, for evermore
On the life that was before.

And the friend who knows him best
Sees him as he sees the rest
Who are striving to be wise
While a Demon's arms and eyes
Hold them as a web would flies.

All the words of all the world,
Aimed together and then hurled,
Would be stiller in his ears
Than a closing of still shears
On a thread made out of years.

But there lives another sound,
More compelling, more profound;
There's a music, so it seems,
That assuages and redeems,
More than reason, more than dreams.

There's a music yet unheard
By the creature of the word,
Though it matters little more
Than a wave-wash on a shore—
Till a Demon shuts a door.

So, if he be very still
With his Demon, and one will,
Murmurs of it may be blown
To my friend who is alone
In a room that I have known.

After that from everywhere
Singing life will find him there;
Then the door will open wide,
And my friend, again outside,
Will be living, having died.

The Poor Relation

No longer torn by what she knows
And sees within the eyes of others,
Her doubts are when the daylight goes,
Her fears are for the few she bothers.
She tells them it is wholly wrong
Of her to stay alive so long;
And when she smiles her forehead shows
A crinkle that had been her mother's.

Beneath her beauty, blanched with pain,
And wistful yet for being cheated,
A child would seem to ask again
A question many times repeated;
But no rebellion has betrayed
Her wonder at what she has paid
For memories that have no stain,
For triumph born to be defeated.

To those who come for what she was—
The few left who know where to find her—
She clings, for they are all she has;
And she may smile when they remind her,
As heretofore, of what they know

Of roses that are still to blow
By ways where not so much as grass
Remains of what she sees behind her.

They stay a while, and having done
What penance or the past requires,
They go, and leave her there alone
To count her chimneys and her spires.
Her lip shakes when they go away,
And yet she would not have them stay;
She knows as well as anyone
That Pity, having played, soon tires.

But one friend always reappears,
A good ghost, not to be forsaken;
Whereat she laughs and has no fears
Of what a ghost may reawaken,
But welcomes, while she wears and mends
The poor relation's odds and ends,
Her truant from a tomb of years—
Her power of youth so early taken.

Poor laugh, more slender than her song
It seems; and there are none to hear it
With even the stopped ears of the strong
For breaking heart or broken spirit.
The friends who clamored for her place,
And would have scratched her for her face,
Have lost her laughter for so long
That none would care enough to fear it.

None live who need fear anything
From her, whose losses are their pleasure;
The plover with a wounded wing

Stays not the flight that others measure;
So there she waits, and while she lives,
And death forgets, and faith forgives,
Her memories go foraging
For bits of childhood song they treasure.

And like a giant harp that hums
On always, and is always blending
The coming of what never comes
With what has past and had an ending,
The City trembles, throbs, and pounds
Outside, and through a thousand sounds
The small intolerable drums
Of Time are like slow drops descending.

Bereft enough to shame a sage
And given little to long sighing,
With no illusion to assuage
The lonely changelessness of dying,—
Unsought, unthought-of, and unheard,
She sings and watches like a bird,
Safe in a comfortable cage
From which there will be no more flying.

Fragment

Faint white pillars that seem to fade
As you look from here are the first one sees
Of his house where it hides and dies in a shade
Of beeches and oaks and hickory trees.
Now many a man, given woods like these,

And a house like that, and the Briony gold,
Would have said, "There are still some gods to please,
And houses are built without hands, we're told."

There are the pillars, and all gone gray.
Briony's hair went white. You may see
Where the garden was if you come this way.
That sun-dial scared him, he said to me;
"Sooner or later they strike," said he,
And he never got that from the books he read.
Others are flourishing, worse than he,
But he knew too much for the life he led.

And who knows all knows everything
That a patient ghost at last retrieves;
There's more to be known of his harvesting
When Time the thresher unbinds the sheaves;
And there's more to be heard than a wind that grieves
For Briony now in this ageless oak,
Driving the first of its withered leaves
Over the stones where the fountain broke.

Bewick Finzer

Time was when his half million drew
    The breath of six per cent;
But soon the worm of what-was-not
    Fed hard on his content;
And something crumbled in his brain
    When his half million went.

Time passed, and filled along with his
    The place of many more;
Time came, and hardly one of us
    Had credence to restore,
From what appeared one day, the man
    Whom we had known before.

The broken voice, the withered neck,
    The coat worn out with care,
The cleanliness of indigence,
    The brilliance of despair,
The fond imponderable dreams
    Of affluence,—all were there.

Poor Finzer, with his dreams and schemes,
    Fares hard now in the race,
With heart and eye that have a task
    When he looks in the face
Of one who might so easily
    Have been in Finzer's place.

He comes unfailing for the loan
    We give and then forget;
He comes, and probably for years
    Will he be coming yet,—
Familiar as an old mistake,
    And futile as regret.

Bokardo

Well, Bokardo, here we are;
    Make yourself at home.
Look around—you haven't far
    To look—and why be dumb?
Not the place that used to be,
Not so many things to see;
But there's room for you and me.
    And you—you've come.

Talk a little; or, if not,
    Show me with a sign
Why it was that you forgot
    What was yours and mine.
Friends, I gather, are small things
In an age when coins are kings;
Even at that, one hardly flings
    Friends before swine.

Rather strong? I knew as much,
    For it made you speak.
No offense to swine, as such,
    But why this hide-and-seek?
You have something on your side,
And you wish you might have died,
So you tell me. And you tried
    One night last week?

You tried hard? And even then
    Found a time to pause?
When you try as hard again,
    You'll have another cause.
When you find yourself at odds

With all dreamers of all gods,
You may smite yourself with rods—
    But not the laws.

Though they seem to show a spite
    Rather devilish,
They move on as with a might
    Stronger than your wish.
Still, however strong they be,
They bide man's authority:
Xerxes, when he flogged the sea,
    May've scared a fish.

It's a comfort, if you like,
    To keep honor warm,
But as often as you strike
    The laws, you do no harm.
To the laws, I mean. To you—
That's another point of view,
One you may as well indue
    With some alarm.

Not the most heroic face
    To present, I grant;
Nor will you insure disgrace
    By fearing what you want
Freedom has a world of sides,
And if reason once derides
Courage, then your courage hides
    A deal of cant.

Learn a little to forget
    Life was once a feast;
You aren't fit for dying yet,

So don't be a beast.
Few men with a mind will say,
Thinking twice, that they can pay
Half their debts of yesterday,
        Or be released.

There's a debt now on your mind
        More than any gold?
And there's nothing you can find
        Out there in the cold?
Only—what's his name?—Remorse?
And Death riding on his horse?
Well, be glad there's nothing worse
        Than you have told.

Leave Remorse to warm his hands
        Outside in the rain.
As for Death, he understands,
        And he will come again.
Therefore, till your wits are clear,
Flourish and be quiet—here.
But a devil at each ear
        Will be a strain?

Past a doubt they will indeed,
        More than you have earned.
I say that because you need
        Ablution, being burned?
Well, if you must have it so,
Your last flight went rather low.
Better say you had to know
        What you have learned.

And that's over. Here you are,
 Battered by the past.
Time will have his little scar,
 But the wound won't last.
Nor shall harrowing surprise
Find a world without its eyes
If a star fades when the skies
 Are overcast.

God knows there are lives enough,
 Crushed, and too far gone
Longer to make sermons of,
 And those we leave alone.
Others, if they will, may rend
The worn patience of a friend
Who, though smiling, sees the end,
 With nothing done.

But your fervor to be free
 Fled the faith it scorned;
Death demands a decency
 Of you, and you are warned.
But for all we give we get
Mostly blows? Don't be upset;
You, Bokardo, are not yet
 Consumed or mourned.

There'll be falling into view
 Much to rearrange;
And there'll be a time for you
 To marvel at the change.
They that have the least to fear

Question hardest what is here;
When long-hidden skies are clear,
The stars look strange.

Isaac and Archibald

(TO MRS. HENRY RICHARDS)

Isaac and Archibald were two old men.
I knew them, and I may have laughed at them
A little; but I must have honored them
For they were old, and they were good to me.

I do not think of either of them now,
Without remembering, infallibly,
A journey that I made one afternoon
With Isaac to find out what Archibald
Was doing with his oats. It was high time
Those oats were cut, said Isaac; and he feared
That Archibald—well, he could never feel
Quite sure of Archibald. Accordingly
The good old man invited me—that is,
Permitted me—to go along with him;
And I, with a small boy's adhesiveness
To competent old age, got up and went.
I do not know that I cared overmuch
For Archibald's or anybody's oats,
But Archibald was quite another thing,
And Isaac yet another; and the world
Was wide, and there was gladness everywhere.
We walked together down the River Road
With all the warmth and wonder of the land
Around us, and the wayside flash of leaves,—

And Isaac said the day was glorious;
But somewhere at the end of the first mile
I found that I was figuring to find
How long those ancient legs of his would keep
The pace that he had set for them. The sun
Was hot, and I was ready to sweat blood;
But Isaac, for aught I could make of him,
Was cool to his hat-band. So I said then
With a dry gasp of affable despair,
Something about the scorching days we have
In August without knowing it sometimes;
But Isaac said the day was like a dream,
And praised the Lord, and talked about the breeze.
I made a fair confession of the breeze,
And crowded casually on his thought
The nearness of a profitable nook
That I could see. First I was half inclined
To caution him that he was growing old,
But something that was not compassion soon
Made plain the folly of all subterfuge.
Isaac was old, but not so old as that.

So I proposed, without an overture,
That we be seated in the shade a while,
And Isaac made no murmur. Soon the talk
Was turned on Archibald, and I began
To feel some premonitions of a kind
That only childhood knows; for the old man
Had looked at me and clutched me with his eye,
And asked if I had ever noticed things.
I told him that I could not think of them,
And I knew then, by the frown that left his face
Unsatisfied, that I had injured him.
"My good young friend," he said, "you cannot feel

What I have seen so long. You have the eyes—
Oh, yes—but you have not the other things:
The sight within that never will deceive,
You do not know—you have no right to know;
The twilight warning of experience,
The singular idea of loneliness,—
These are not yours. But they have long been mine,
And they have shown me now for seven years
That Archibald is changing. It is not
So much that he should come to his last hand,
And leave the game, and go the old way down;
But I have known him in and out so long,
And I have seen so much of good in him
That other men have shared and have not seen,
And I have gone so far through thick and thin,
Through cold and fire with him, that now it brings
To this old heart of mine an ache that you
Have not yet lived enough to know about.
But even unto you, and your boy's faith,
Your freedom, and your untried confidence,
A time will come to find out what it means
To know that you are losing what was yours,
To know that you are being left behind;
And then the long contempt of innocence—
God bless you, boy!—don't think the worse of it
Because an old man chatters in the shade—
Will all be like a story you have read
In childhood and remembered for the pictures.
And when the best friend of your life goes down,
When first you know in him the slackening
That comes, and coming always tells the end,—
Now in a common word that would have passed
Uncaught from any other lips than his,
Now in some trivial act of every day,

Done as he might have done it all along
But for a twinging little difference
That nips you like a squirrel's teeth—oh, yes,
Then you will understand it well enough.
But oftener it comes in other ways;
It comes without your knowing when it comes;
You know that he is changing, and you know
That he is going—just as I know now
That Archibald is going, and that I
Am staying . . . Look at me, my boy,
And when the time shall come for you to see
That I must follow after him, try then
To think of me, to bring me back again,
Just as I was to-day. Think of the place
Where we are sitting now, and think of me—
Think of old Isaac as you knew him then,
When you set out with him in August once
To see old Archibald."—The words come back
Almost as Isaac must have uttered them,
And there comes with them a dry memory
Of something in my throat that would not move.

If you had asked me then to tell just why
I made so much of Isaac and the things
He said, I should have gone far for an answer;
For I knew it was not sorrow that I felt,
Whatever I may have wished it, or tried then
To make myself believe. My mouth was full
Of words, and they would have been comforting
To Isaac, spite of my twelve years, I think;
But there was not in me the willingness
To speak them out. Therefore I watched the ground;
And I was wondering what made the Lord
Create a thing so nervous as an ant,

When Isaac, with commendable unrest,
Ordained that we should take the road again—
For it was yet three miles to Archibald's,
And one to the first pump. I felt relieved
All over when the old man told me that;
I felt that he had stilled a fear of mine
That those extremities of heat and cold
Which he had long gone through with Archibald
Had made the man impervious to both;
But Isaac had a desert somewhere in him,
And at the pump he thanked God for all things
That He had put on earth for men to drink,
And he drank well,—so well that I proposed
That we go slowly lest I learn too soon
The bitterness of being left behind,
And all those other things. That was a joke
To Isaac, and it pleased him very much;
And that pleased me—for I was twelve years old.

At the end of an hour's walking after that
The cottage of old Archibald appeared.
Little and white and high on a smooth round hill
It stood, with hackmatacks and apple-trees
Before it, and a big barn-roof beyond;
And over the place—trees, houses, fields and all—
Hovered an air of still simplicity
And a fragrance of old summers—the old style
That lives the while it passes. I dare say
That I was lightly conscious of all this
When Isaac, of a sudden, stopped himself,
And for the long first quarter of a minute
Gazed with incredulous eyes, forgetful quite
Of breezes and of me and of all else
Under the scorching sun but a smooth-cut field,

Faint yellow in the distance. I was young,
But there were a few things that I could see,
And this was one of them.—"Well, well!" said he;
And "Archibald will be surprised, I think,"
Said I. But all my childhood subtlety
Was lost on Isaac, for he strode along
Like something out of Homer—powerful
And awful on the wayside, so I thought.
Also I thought how good it was to be
So near the end of my short-legged endeavor
To keep the pace with Isaac for five miles.

Hardly had we turned in from the main road
When Archibald, with one hand on his back
And the other clutching his huge-headed cane,
Came limping down to meet us.—"Well! well! well!"
Said he; and then he looked at my red face,
All streaked with dust and sweat, and shook my hand,
And said it must have been a right smart walk
That we had had that day from Tilbury Town.—
"Magnificent," said Isaac; and he told
About the beautiful west wind there was
Which cooled and clarified the atmosphere.
"You must have made it with your legs, I guess,"
Said Archibald; and Isaac humored him
With one of those infrequent smiles of his
Which he kept in reserve, apparently,
For Archibald alone. "But why," said he,
"Should Providence have cider in the world
If not for such an afternoon as this?"
And Archibald, with a soft light in his eyes,
Replied that if he chose to go down cellar,
There he would find eight barrels—one of which
Was newly tapped, he said, and to his taste

An honor to the fruit. Isaac approved
Most heartily of that, and guided us
Forthwith, as if his venerable feet
Were measuring the turf in his own door-yard,
Straight to the open rollway. Down we went,
Out of the fiery sunshine to the gloom,
Grateful and half sepulchral, where we found
The barrels, like eight potent sentinels,
Close ranged along the wall. From one of them
A bright pine spile stuck out alluringly,
And on the black flat stone, just under it,
Glimmered a late-spilled proof that Archibald
Had spoken from unfeigned experience.
There was a fluted antique water-glass
Close by, and in it, prisoned, or at rest,
There was a cricket, of the brown soft sort
That feeds on darkness. Isaac turned him out,
And touched him with his thumb to make him jump,
And then composedly pulled out the plug
With such a practised hand that scarce a drop
Did even touch his fingers. Then he drank
And smacked his lips with a slow patronage
And looked along the line of barrels there
With a pride that may have been forgetfulness
That they were Archibald's and not his own.
"I never twist a spigot nowadays,"
He said, and raised the glass up to the light,
"But I thank God for orchards." And that glass
Was filled repeatedly for the same hand
Before I thought it worth while to discern
Again that I was young, and that old age,
With all his woes, had some advantages.

"Now, Archibald," said Isaac, when we stood
Outside again, "I have it in my mind
That I shall take a sort of little walk—
To stretch my legs and see what you are doing.
You stay and rest your back and tell the boy
A story: Tell him all about the time
In Stafford's cabin forty years ago,
When four of us were snowed up for ten days
With only one dried haddock. Tell him all
About it, and be wary of your back.
Now I will go along."—I looked up then
At Archibald, and as I looked I saw
Just how his nostrils widened once or twice
And then grew narrow. I can hear to-day
The way the old man chuckled to himself—
Not wholesomely, not wholly to convince
Another of his mirth,—as I can hear
The lonely sigh that followed.—But at length
He said: "The orchard now's the place for us;
We may find something like an apple there,
And we shall have the shade, at any rate."
So there we went and there we laid ourselves
Where the sun could not reach us; and I champed
A dozen of worm-blighted astrakhans
While Archibald said nothing—merely told
The tale of Stafford's cabin, which was good,
Though "master chilly"—after his own phrase—
Even for a day like that. But other thoughts
Were moving in his mind, imperative,
And writhing to be spoken: I could see
The glimmer of them in a glance or two,
Cautious, or else unconscious, that he gave
Over his shoulder:... "Stafford and the rest—
But that's an old song now, and Archibald

And Isaac are old men. Remember, boy,
That we are old. Whatever we have gained,
Or lost, or thrown away, we are old men.
You look before you and we look behind,
And we are playing life out in the shadow—
But that's not all of it. The sunshine lights
A good road yet before us if we look,
And we are doing that when least we know it;
For both of us are children of the sun,
Like you, and like the weed there at your feet.
The shadow calls us, and it frightens us—
We think; but there's a light behind the stars
And we old fellows who have dared to live,
We see it—and we see the other things,
The other things . . . Yes, I have seen it come
These eight years, and these ten years, and I know
Now that it cannot be for very long
That Isaac will be Isaac. You have seen—
Young as you are, you must have seen the strange
Uncomfortable habit of the man?
He'll take my nerves and tie them in a knot
Sometimes, and that's not Isaac. I know that—
And I know what it is: I get it here
A little, in my knees, and Isaac—here."
The old man shook his head regretfully
And laid his knuckles three times on his forehead.
"That's what it is: Isaac is not quite right.
You see it, but you don't know what it means:
The thousand little differences—no,
You do not know them, and it's well you don't;
You'll know them soon enough—God bless you, boy!—
You'll know them, but not all of them—not all.
So think of them as little as you can:
There's nothing in them for you, or for me—

But I am old and I must think of them;
I'm in the shadow, but I don't forget
The light, my boy,—the light behind the stars.
Remember that: remember that I said it;
And when the time that you think far away
Shall come for you to say it—say it, boy;
Let there be no confusion or distrust
In you, no snarling of a life half lived,
Nor any cursing over broken things
That your complaint has been the ruin of.
Live to see clearly and the light will come
To you, and as you need it.—But there, there,
I'm going it again, as Isaac says,
And I'll stop now before you go to sleep.—
Only be sure that you growl cautiously,
And always where the shadow may not reach you."

Never shall I forget, long as I live,
The quaint thin crack in Archibald's voice,
The lonely twinkle in his little eyes,
Or the way it made me feel to be with him.
I know I lay and looked for a long time
Down through the orchard and across the road,
Across the river and the sun-scorched hills
That ceased in a blue forest, where the world
Ceased with it. Now and then my fancy caught
A flying glimpse of a good life beyond—
Something of ships and sunlight, streets and singing,
Troy falling, and the ages coming back,
And ages coming forward: Archibald
And Isaac were good fellows in old clothes,
And Agememnon was a friend of mine;

Ulysses coming home again to shoot
With bows and feathered arrows made another,
And all was as it should be. I was young.

So I lay dreaming of what things I would,
Calm and incorrigibly satisfied
With apples and romance and ignorance,
And the still smoke from Archibald's clay pipe.
There was a stillness over everything,
As if the spirit of heat had laid its hand
Upon the world and hushed it; and I felt
Within the mightiness of the white sun
That smote the land around us and wrought out
A fragrance from the trees, a vital warmth
And fullness for the time that was to come,
And a glory for the world beyond the forest.
The present and the future and the past,
Isaac and Archibald, the burning bush,
The Trojans and the walls of Jericho,
Were beautifully fused; and all went well
Till Archibald began to fret for Isaac
And said it was a master day for sunstroke.
That was enough to make a mummy smile,
I thought; and I remained hilarious,
In face of all precedence and respect,
Till Isaac (who had come to us unheard)
Found he had no tobacco, looked at me
Peculiarly, and asked of Archibald
What ailed the boy to make him chirrup so.
From that he told us what a blessed world
The Lord had given us.—"But, Archibald,"
He added, with a sweet severity
That made me think of peach-skins and goose-flesh,
"I'm half afraid you cut those oats of yours

A day or two before they were well set."
"They were set well enough," said Archibald,—
And I remarked the process of his nose
Before the words came out. "But never mind
Your neighbor's oats: you stay here in the shade
And rest yourself while I go find the cards.
We'll have a little game of seven-up
And let the boy keep count."—"We'll have the game,
Assuredly," said Isaac; "and I think
That I will have a drop of cider, also."

They marched away together towards the house
And left me to my childish ruminations
Upon the ways of men. I followed them
Down cellar with my fancy, and then left them
For a fairer vision of all things at once
That was anon to be destroyed again
By the sound of voices and of heavy feet—
One of the sounds of life that I remember,
Though I forget so many that rang first
As if they were thrown down to me from Sinai.

So I remember, even to this day,
Just how they sounded, how they placed themselves,
And how the game went on while I made marks
And crossed them out, and meanwhile made some Trojans.
Likewise I made Ulysses, after Isaac,
And a little after Flaxman. Archibald
Was injured when he found himself left out,
But he had no heroics, and I said so:
I told him that his white beard was too long
And too straight down to be like things in Homer.
"Quite so," said Isaac.—"Low," said Archibald;
And he threw down a deuce with a deep grin

That showed his yellow teeth and made me happy.
So they played on till a bell rang from the door,
And Archibald said, "Supper."—After that
The old men smoked while I sat watching them
And wondered with all comfort what might come
To me, and what might never come to me;
And when the time came for the long walk home
With Isaac in the twilight, I could see
The forest and the sunset and the sky-line,
No matter where it was that I was looking:
The flame beyond the boundary, the music,
The foam and the white ships, and two old men
Were things that would not leave me.—And that night
There came to me a dream—a shining one,
With two old angels in it. They had wings,
And they were sitting where a silver light
Suffused them, face to face. The wings of one
Began to palpitate as I approached,
But I was yet unseen when a dry voice
Cried thinly, with unpatronizing triumph,
"I've got you, Isaac; high, low, jack, and the game."

Isaac and Archibald have gone their way
To the silence of the loved and well-forgotten.
I knew them, and I may have laughed at them;
But there's a laughing that has honor in it,
And I have no regret for light words now.
Rather I think sometimes they may have made
Their sport of me;—but they would not do that,
They were too old for that. They were old men,
And I may laugh at them because I knew them.

Aunt Imogen

Aunt Imogen was coming, and therefore
The children—Jane, Sylvester, and Young George—
Were eyes and ears; for there was only one
Aunt Imogen to them in the whole world,
And she was in it only for four weeks
In fifty-two. But those great bites of time
Made all September a Queen's Festival;
And they would strive, informally, to make
The most of them.—The mother understood,
And wisely stepped away. Aunt Imogen
Was there for only one month in the year,
While she, the mother,—she was always there;
And that was what made all the difference.
She knew it must be so, for Jane had once
Expounded it to her so learnedly
That she had looked away from the child's eyes
And thought; and she had thought of many things.

There was a demonstration every time
Aunt Imogen appeared, and there was more
Than one this time. And she was at a loss
Just how to name the meaning of it all:
It puzzled her to think that she could be
So much to any crazy thing alive—
Even to her sister's little savages
Who knew no better than to be themselves;
But in the midst of her glad wonderment
She found herself besieged and overcome
By two tight arms and one tumultuous head.
And therewith half bewildered and half pained
By the joy she felt and by the sudden love
That proved itself in childhood's honest noise.

Jane, by the wings of sex, had reached her first;
And while she strangled her, approvingly,
Sylvester thumped his drum and Young George howled.
But finally, when all was rectified,
And she had stilled the clamor of Young George
By giving him a long ride on her shoulders,
They went together into the old room
That looked across the fields; and Imogen
Gazed out with a girl's gladness in her eyes,
Happy to know that she was back once more
Where there were those who knew her, and at last
Had gloriously got away again
From cabs and clattered asphalt for a while;
And there she sat and talked and looked and laughed
And made the mother and the children laugh.
Aunt Imogen made everybody laugh.

There was the feminine paradox—that she
Who had so little sunshine for herself
Should have so much for others. How it was
That she could make, and feel for making it,
So much of joy for them, and all along
Be covering, like a scar, and while she smiled,
That hungering incompleteness and regret—
That passionate ache for something of her own,
For something of herself—she never knew.
She knew that she could seem to make them all
Believe there was no other part of her
Than her persistent happiness; but the why
And how she did not know. Still none of them
Could have a thought that she was living down—
Almost as if regret were criminal,
So proud it was and yet so profitless—
The penance of a dream, and that was good.

Her sister Jane—the mother of little Jane,
Sylvester, and Young George—might make herself
Believe she knew, for she—well, she was Jane.

Young George, however, did not yield himself
To nourish the false hunger of a ghost
That made no good return. He saw too much:
The accumulated wisdom of his years
Had so conclusively made plain to him
The permanent profusion of a world
Where everybody might have everything
To do, and almost everything to eat,
That he was jubilantly satisfied
And all unthwarted by adversity.
Young George knew things. The world, he had found out,
Was a good place, and life was a good game—
Particularly when Aunt Imogen
Was in it. And one day it came to pass—
One rainy day when she was holding him
And rocking him—that he, in his own right,
Took it upon himself to tell her so;
And something in his way of telling it—
The language, or the tone, or something else—
Gripped like insidious fingers on her throat,
And then went foraging as if to make
A plaything of her heart. Such undeserved
And unsophisticated confidence
Went mercilessly home; and had she sat
Before a looking glass, the deeps of it
Could not have shown more clearly to her then
Than one thought-mirrored little glimpse had shown
The pang that wrenched her face and filled her eyes
With anguish and intolerable mist.
The blow that she had vaguely thrust aside

Like fright so many times had found her now:
Clean-thrust and final it had come to her
From a child's lips at last, as it had come
Never before, and as it might be felt
Never again. Some grief, like some delight,
Stings hard but once: to custom after that
The rapture or the pain submits itself,
And we are wiser than we were before.
And Imogen was wiser; though at first
Her dream-defeating wisdom was indeed
A thankless heritage: there was no sweet,
No bitter now; nor was there anything
To make a daily meaning for her life—
Till truth, like Harlequin, leapt out somehow
From ambush and threw sudden savor to it—
But the blank taste of time. There were no dreams,
No phantoms in her future any more:
One clinching revelation of what was
One by-flash of irrevocable chance,
Had acridly but honestly foretold
The mystical fulfilment of a life
That might have once . . . But that was all gone by:
There was no need of reaching back for that:
The triumph was not hers: there was no love
Save borrowed love: there was no might have been.

But there was yet Young George—and he had gone
Conveniently to sleep, like a good boy;
And there was yet Sylvester and his drum,
And there was frowzle-headed little Jane;
And there was Jane the sister, and the mother,—
Her sister, and the mother of them all.
They were not hers, not even one of them:
She was not born to be so much as that,

For she was born to be Aunt Imogen.
Now she could see the truth and look at it;
Now she could make stars out where once had palled
A future's emptiness; now she could share
With others—ah, the others!—to the end
The largess of a woman who could smile;
Now it was hers to dance the folly down,
And all the murmuring; now it was hers
To be Aunt Imogen.—So, when Young George
Woke up and blinked at her with his big eyes,
And smiled to see the way she blinked at him,
'T was only in old concord with the stars
That she took hold of him and held him close,
Close to herself, and crushed him till he laughed.

The Growth of "Lorraine"

I

While I stood listening, discreetly dumb,
Lorraine was having the last word with me:
"I know," she said, "I know it, but you see
Some creatures are born fortunate, and some
Are born to be found out and overcome,—
Born to be slaves, to let the rest go free;
And if I'm one of them (and I must be)
You may as well forget me and go home.

"You tell me not to say these things, I know,
But I should never try to be content:
I've gone too far; the life would be too slow.

Some could have done it—some girls have the stuff;
But I can't do it: I don't know enough.
I'm going to the devil."—And she went.

II

I did not half believe her when she said
That I should never hear from her again;
Nor when I found a letter from Lorraine,
Was I surprised or grieved at what I read:
"Dear friend, when you find this, I shall be dead.
You are too far away to make me stop.
They say that one drop—think of it, one drop!—
Will be enough,—but I'll take five instead.

"You do not frown because I call you friend,
For I would have you glad that I still keep
Your memory, and even at the end—
Impenitent, sick, shattered—cannot curse
The love that flings, for better or for worse,
This worn-out, cast-out flesh of mine to sleep."

Erasmus

When he protested, not too solemnly,
That for a world's achieving maintenance
The crust of overdone divinity
Lacked aliment, they called it recreance;
And when he chose through his own glass to scan
Sick Europe, and reduced, unyieldingly,
The monk within the cassock to the man
Within the monk, they called it heresy.

And when he made so perilously bold
As to be scattered forth in black and white,
Good fathers looked askance at him and rolled
Their inward eyes in anguish and affright;
There were some of them did shake at what was told,
And they shook best who knew that he was right.

The Woman and the Wife

I—THE EXPLANATION

"You thought we knew," she said, "but we were wrong.
This we can say, the rest we do not say;
Nor do I let you throw yourself away
Because you love me. Let us both be strong,
And we shall find in sorrow, before long,
Only the price Love ruled that we should pay:
The dark is at the end of every day,
And silence is the end of every song.

"You ask me for one proof that I speak right,
But I can answer only what I know;
You look for just one lie to make black white,
But I can tell you only what is true—
God never made me for the wife of you.
This we can say,—believe me!... Tell me so!"

II—THE ANNIVERSARY

"Give me the truth, whatever it may be.
You thought we knew, now tell me what you miss:
You are the one to tell me what it is—
You are a man, and you have married me.

What is it worth to-night that you can see
More marriage in the dream of one dead kiss
Than in a thousand years of life like this?
Passion has turned the lock, Pride keeps the key.

"Whatever I have said or left unsaid,
Whatever I have done or left undone,—
Tell me. Tell me the truth. . . . Are you afraid?
Do you think that Love was ever fed with lies
But hunger lived thereafter in his eyes?
Do you ask me to take moonlight for the sun?"

from *Merlin (the conclusion)*

                                   Merlin smiled,
Faintly, and for the moment: "Dagonet,
I need your word as one of Arthur's knights
That you will go on with me to the end
Of my short way, and say unto no man
Or woman that you found or saw me here.
No good would follow, for a doubt would live
Unstifled of my loyalty to him
Whose deeds are wrought for those who are to come;
And many who see not what I have seen,
Or what you see tonight, would prattle on
For ever, and their children after them,
Of what might once have been had I gone down
With you to Camelot to see the King.
I came to see the King,—but why see kings?
All this that was to be is what I saw
Before there was an Arthur to be king,
And so to be a mirror wherein men
May see themselves, and pause. If they see not,

Or if they do see and they ponder not,—
I saw; but I was neither Fate nor God.
I saw too much; and this would be the end,
Were there to be an end. I saw myself—
A sight no other man has ever seen;
And through the dark that lay beyond myself
I saw two fires that are to light the world."

On Dagonet the silent hand of Merlin
Weighed now as living iron that held him down
With a primeval power. Doubt, wonderment,
Impatience, and a self-accusing sorrow
Born of an ancient love, possessed and held him
Until his love was more than he could name,
And he was Merlin's fool, not Arthur's now:
"Say what you will, I say that I'm the fool
Of Merlin, King of Nowhere; which is Here.
With you for king and me for court, what else
Have we to sigh for but a place to sleep?
I know a tavern that will take us in;
And on the morrow I shall follow you
Until I die for you. And when I die . . ."—
"Well, Dagonet, the King is listening."—
And Dagonet answered, hearing in the words
Of Merlin a grave humor and a sound
Of graver pity, "I shall die a fool."
He heard what might have been a father's laugh,
Faintly behind him; and the living weight
Of Merlin's hand was lifted. They arose,
And, saying nothing, found a groping way
Down through the gloom together. Fiercer now,
The wind was like a flying animal
That beat the two of them incessantly
With icy wings, and bit them as they went.

The rock above them was an empty place
Where neither seer nor fool should view again
The stricken city. Colder blew the wind
Across the world, and on it heavier lay
The shadow and the burden of the night;
And there was darkness over Camelot.

The Master

(Lincoln)

A flying word from here and there
Had sown the name at which we sneered,
But soon the name was everywhere,
To be reviled and then revered:
A presence to be loved and feared,
We cannot hide it, or deny
That we, the gentlemen who jeered,
May be forgotten by and by.

He came when days were perilous
And hearts of men were sore beguiled;
And having made his note of us,
He pondered and was reconciled.
Was ever master yet so mild
As he, and so untamable?
We doubted, even when he smiled,
Not knowing what he knew so well.

He knew that undeceiving fate
Would shame us whom he served unsought;
He knew that he must wince and wait—
The jest of those for whom he fought;

He knew devoutly what he thought
Of us and of our ridicule;
He knew that we must all be taught
Like little children in a school.

We gave a glamour to the task
That he encountered and saw through,
But little of us did he ask,
And little did we ever do.
And what appears if we review
The season when we railed and chaffed?
It is the face of one who knew
That we were learning while we laughed.

The face that in our vision feels
Again the venom that we flung,
Transfigured to the world reveals
The vigilance to which we clung.
Shrewd, hallowed, harassed, and among
The mysteries that are untold,
The face we see was never young
Nor could it wholly have been old.

For he, to whom we had applied
Our shopman's test of age and worth,
Was elemental when he died,
As he was ancient at his birth:
The saddest among kings of earth,
Bowed with a galling crown, this man
Met rancor with a cryptic mirth,
Laconic—and Olympian.

The love, the grandeur, and the fame
Are bounded by the world alone;
The calm, the smouldering, and the flame
Of awful patience were his own:
With him they are forever flown
Past all our fond self-shadowings,
Wherewith we cumber the Unknown
As with inept, Icarian wings.

For we were not as other men:
'Twas ours to soar and his to see;
But we are coming down again,
And we shall come down pleasantly;
Nor shall we longer disagree
On what it is to be sublime,
But flourish in our perigee
And have one Titan at a time.

Calverly's

We go no more to Calverly's,
For there the lights are few and low;
And who are there to see by them,
Or what they see, we do not know.
Poor strangers of another tongue
May now creep in from anywhere,
And we, forgotten, be no more
Than twilight on a ruin there.

We two, the remnant. All the rest
Are cold and quiet. You nor I,
Nor fiddle now, nor flagon-lid,
May ring them back from where they lie.

No fame delays oblivion
For them, but something yet survives:
A record written fair, could we
But read the book of scattered lives.

There'll be a page for Leffingwell,
And one for Lingard, the Moon-calf;
And who knows what for Clavering,
Who died because he couldn't laugh?
Who knows or cares? No sign is here,
No face, no voice, no memory;
No Lingard with his eerie joy,
No Clavering, no Calverly.

We cannot have them here with us
To say where their light lives are gone,
Or if they be of other stuff
Than are the moons of Ilion.
So, be their place of one estate
With ashes, echoes, and old wars,—
Or ever we be of the night,
Or we be lost among the stars.

Uncle Ananias

His words were magic and his heart was true,
  And everywhere he wandered he was blessed.
Out of all ancient men my childhood knew
  I choose him and I mark him for the best.
Of all authoritative liars, too,
  I crown him loveliest.

How fondly I remember the delight
    That always glorified him in the spring;
The joyous courage and the benedight
    Profusion of his faith in everything!
He was a good old man, and it was right
    That he should have his fling.

And often, underneath the apple-trees,
    When we surprised him in the summer time,
With what superb magnificence and ease
    He sinned enough to make the day sublime!
And if he liked us there about his knees,
    Truly it was no crime.

All summer long we loved him for the same
    Perennial inspiration of his lies;
And when the russet wealth of autumn came,
    There flew but fairer visions to our eyes—
Multiple, tropical, winged with a feathery flame,
    Like birds of paradise.

So to the sheltered end of many a year
    He charmed the seasons out with pageantry
Wearing upon his forehead, with no fear,
    The laurel of approved iniquity.
And every child who knew him, far or near,
    Did love him faithfully.

The Whip

The doubt you fought so long
The cynic net you cast,
The tyranny, the wrong,
The ruin, they are past;
And here you are at last,
Your blood no longer vexed.
The coffin has you fast,
The clod will have you next.

But fear you not the clod,
Nor ever doubt the grave:
The roses and the sod
Will not forswear the wave.
The gift the river gave
Is now but theirs to cover:
The mistress and the slave
Are gone now, and the lover.

You left the two to find
Their own way to the brink
Then—shall I call you blind?—
You chose to plunge and sink.
God knows the gall we drink
Is not the mead we cry for,
Nor was it, I should think—
For you—a thing to die for.

Could we have done the same,
Had we been in your place?—
This funeral of your name
Throws no light on the case.
Could we have made the chase,

And felt then as you felt?—
But what's this on your face,
Blue, curious, like a welt?

There were some ropes of sand
Recorded long ago,
But none, I understand,
Of water. Is it so?
And she—she struck the blow,
You but a neck behind . . .
You saw the river flow—
Still, shall I call you blind?

The White Lights

(Broadway, 1906)

When in from Delos came the gold
That held the dream of Pericles,
When first Athenian ears were told
The tumult of Euripides,
When men met Aristophanes,
Who fledged them with immortal quills—
Here, where the time knew none of these,
There were some islands and some hills.

When Rome went ravening to see
The sons of mothers end their days,
When Flaccus bade Leuconoë
To banish her Chaldean ways,
When first the pearled, alembic phrase

Of Maro into music ran—
Here there was neither blame nor praise
For Rome, or for the Mantuan.

When Avon, like a faery floor,
Lay freighted, for the eyes of One,
With galleons laden long before
By moonlit wharves in Avalon—
Here, where the white lights have begun
To seethe a way for something fair,
No prophet knew, from what was done,
That there was triumph in the air.

Exit

For what we owe to other days,
Before we poisoned him with praise,
May we who shrank to find him weak
Remember that he cannot speak.

For envy that we may recall,
And for our faith before the fall,
May we who are alive be slow
To tell what we shall never know.

For penance he would not confess,
And for the fateful emptiness
Of early triumph undermined,
May we now venture to be kind.

Doctor of Billiards

Of all among the fallen from on high,
We count you last and leave you to regain
Your born dominion of a life made vain
By three spheres of insidious ivory.
You dwindle to the lesser tragedy—
Content, you say. We call, but you remain.
Nothing alive gone wrong could be so plain,
Or quite so blasted with absurdity.

You click away the kingdom that is yours,
And you click off your crown for cap and bells;
You smile, who are still master of the feast,
And for your smile we credit you the least;
But when your false, unhallowed laugh occurs,
We seem to think there may be something else.

How Annandale Went Out

"They called it Annandale—and I was there
To flourish, to find words, and to attend:
Liar, physician, hypocrite, and friend,
I watched him; and the sight was not so fair
As one or two that I have seen elsewhere:
An apparatus not for me to mend—
A wreck, with hell between him and the end,
Remained of Annandale; and I was there.

"I knew the ruin as I knew the man;
So put the two together, if you can,
Remembering the worst you know of me.

Now view yourself as I was, on the spot—
With a slight kind of engine. Do you see?
Like this . . . You wouldn't hang me? I thought not."

Miniver Cheevy

Miniver Cheevy, child of scorn,
    Grew lean while he assailed the seasons;
He wept that he was ever born,
    And he had reasons.

Miniver loved the days of old
    When swords were bright and steeds were prancing;
The vision of a warrior bold
    Would set him dancing.

Miniver sighed for what was not,
    And dreamed, and rested from his labors;
He dreamed of Thebes and Camelot,
    And Priam's neighbors.

Miniver mourned the ripe renown
    That made so many a name so fragrant;
He mourned Romance, now on the town,
    And Art, a vagrant.

Miniver loved the Medici,
    Albeit he had never seen one;
He would have sinned incessantly
    Could he have been one.

Miniver cursed the commonplace
    And eyed a khaki suit with loathing;
He missed the mediæval grace
    Of iron clothing.

Miniver scorned the gold he sought,
    But sore annoyed was he without it;
Miniver thought, and thought, and thought,
    And thought about it.

Miniver Cheevy, born too late,
    Scratched his head and kept on thinking;
Miniver coughed, and called it fate,
    And kept on drinking.

Vickery's Mountain

Blue in the west the mountain stands,
    And through the long twilight
Vickery sits with folded hands,
    And Vickery's eyes are bright.

Bright, for he knows what no man else
    On earth as yet may know:
There's a golden word that he never tells,
    And a gift that he will not show.

He dreams of honor and wealth and fame,
    He smiles, and well he may;
For to Vickery once a sick man came
    Who did not go away.

The day before the day to be,
　　"Vickery," said the guest,
"You know as you live what's left of me—
　　And you shall know the rest.

"You know as you live that I have come
　　To this we call the end.
No doubt you have found me troublesome,
　　But you've also found a friend;

"For we shall give and you shall take
　　The gold that is in view;
The mountain there and I shall make
　　A golden man of you.

"And you shall leave a friend behind
　　Who neither frets nor feels;
And you shall move among your kind
　　With hundreds at your heels.

"Now this that I have written here
　　Tells all that need be told;
So, Vickery, take the way that's clear.
　　And be a man of gold."

Vickery turned his eyes again
　　To the far mountain-side,
And wept a tear for worthy men
　　Defeated and defied.

Since then a crafty score of years
　　Have come, and they have gone;
But Vickery counts no lost arrears:
　　He lingers and lives on.

Blue in the west the mountain stands,
 Familiar as a face.
Blue, but Vickery knows what sands
 Are golden at its base.

He dreams and lives upon the day
 When he shall walk with kings.
Vickery smiles—and well he may.
 The life-caged linnet sings.

Vickery thinks the time will come
 To go for what is his;
But hovering, unseen hands at home
 Will hold him where he is.

There's a golden word that he never tells
 And a gift that he will not show.
All to be given to some one else—
 And Vickery not to know.

For a Dead Lady

No more with overflowing light
Shall fill the eyes that now are faded,
Nor shall another's fringe with night
Their woman-hidden world as they did.
No more shall quiver down the days
The flowing wonder of her ways,
Whereof no language may requite
The shifting and the many-shaded.

The grace, divine, definitive,
Clings only as a faint forestalling;
The laugh that love could not forgive
Is hushed, and answers to no calling;
The forehead and the little ears
Have gone where Saturn keeps the years;
The breast where roses could not live
Has done with rising and with falling.

The beauty, shattered by the laws
That have creation in their keeping,
No longer trembles at applause,
Or over children that are sleeping;
And we who delve in beauty's lore
Know all that we have known before
Of what inexorable cause
Makes Time so vicious in his reaping.

Two Gardens in Linndale

Two brothers, Oakes and Oliver,
Two gentle men as ever were,
Would roam no longer, but abide
In Linndale, where their fathers died,
And each would be a gardener.

"Now first we fence the garden through,
With this for me and that for you,"
Said Oliver.—"Divine!" said Oakes,
"And I, while I raise artichokes,
Will do what I was born to do."

"But this is not the soil, you know,"
Said Oliver, "to make them grow:
The parent of us, who is dead,
Compassionately shook his head
Once on a time and told me so."

"I hear you, gentle Oliver,"
Said Oakes, "and in your character
I find as fair a thing indeed
As ever bloomed and ran to seed
Since Adam was a gardener.

"Still, whatsoever I find there,
Forgive me if I do not share
The knowing gloom that you take on
Of one who doubted and is done:
For chemistry meets every prayer."

"Sometimes a rock will meet a plough,"
Said Oliver; "but anyhow
'Tis here we are, 'tis here we live,
With each to take and each to give:
There's no room for a quarrel now.

"I leave you in all gentleness
To science and a ripe success.
Now God be with you, brother Oakes,
With you and with your artichokes:
You have the vision, more or less."

"By fate, that gives to me no choice,
I have the vision and the voice:
Dear Oliver, believe in me,
And we shall see what we shall see;
Henceforward let us both rejoice."

"But first, while we have joy to spare
We'll plant a little here and there;
And if you be not in the wrong,
We'll sing together such a song
As no man yet sings anywhere."

They planted and with fruitful eyes
Attended each his enterprise.
"Now days will come and days will go,
And many a way be found, we know,"
Said Oakes, "and we shall sing, likewise."

"The days will go, the years will go,
And many a song be sung, we know,"
Said Oliver; "and if there be
Good harvesting for you and me,
Who cares if we sing loud or low?"

They planted once, and twice, and thrice,
Like amateurs in paradise;
And every spring, fond, foiled, elate,
Said Oakes, "We are in tune with Fate:
One season longer will suffice."

Year after year 'twas all the same:
With none to envy, none to blame,
They lived along in innocence,
Nor ever once forgot the fence,
Till on a day the Stranger came.

He came to greet them where they were,
And he too was a Gardener:
He stood between these gentle men,
He stayed a little while, and then
The land was all for Oliver.

'Tis Oliver who tills alone
Two gardens that are now his own;
'Tis Oliver who sows and reaps
And listens, while the other sleeps,
For songs undreamed of and unknown.

'Tis he, the gentle anchorite,
Who listens for them day and night;
But most he hears them in the dawn,
When from his trees across the lawn
Birds ring the chorus of the light.

He cannot sing without the voice,
But he may worship and rejoice
For patience in him to remain,
The chosen heir of age and pain,
Instead of Oakes—who had no choice.

'Tis Oliver who sits beside
The other's grave at eventide,
And smokes, and wonders what new race
Will have two gardens, by God's grace,
In Linndale, where their fathers died.

And often, while he sits and smokes,
He sees the ghost of gentle Oakes
Uprooting, with a restless hand,
Soft, shadowy flowers in a land
Of asphodels and artichokes.

The Wandering Jew

I saw by looking in his eyes
That they remembered everything;
And this was how I came to know
That he was here, still wandering.
For though the figure and the scene
Were never to be reconciled,
I knew the man as I had known
His image when I was a child.

With evidence at every turn,
I should have held it safe to guess
That all the newness of New York
Had nothing new in loneliness;
Yet here was one who might be Noah,
Or Nathan, or Abimelech,
Or Lamech, out of ages lost,—
Or, more than all, Melchizedek.

Assured that he was none of these,
I gave them back their names again,
To scan once more those endless eyes
Where all my questions ended then.
I found in them what they revealed
That I shall not live to forget,
And wondered if they found in mine
Compassion that I might regret.

Pity, I learned, was not the least
Of time's offending benefits
That had now for so long impugned
The conservation of his wits:
Rather it was that I should yield,
Alone, the fealty that presents
The tribute of a tempered ear
To an untempered eloquence.

Before I pondered long enough
On whence he came and who he was,
I trembled at his ringing wealth
Of manifold anathemas;
I wondered, while he seared the world,
What new defection ailed the race,
And if it mattered how remote
Our fathers were from such a place.

Before there was an hour for me
To contemplate with less concern
The crumbling realms awaiting us
Than his that was beyond return,
A dawning on the dust of years

Had shaped with an elusive light
Mirages of remembered scenes
That were no longer for the sight.

For now the gloom that hid the man
Became a daylight on his wrath,
And one wherein my fancy viewed
New lions ramping in his path.
The old were dead and had no fangs,
Wherefore he loved them—seeing not
They were the same that in their time
Had eaten everything they caught.

The world around him was a gift
Of anguish to his eyes and ears,
And one that he had long reviled
As fit for devils, not for seers.
Where, then, was there a place for him
That on this other side of death
Saw nothing good, as he had seen
No good come out of Nazareth?

Yet here there was a reticence,
And I believe his only one,
That hushed him as if he beheld
A Presence that would not be gone.
In such a silence he confessed
How much there was to be denied;
And he would look at me and live,
As others might have looked and died.

As if at last he knew again
That he had always known, his eyes
Were like to those of one who gazed

On those of One who never dies.
For such a moment he revealed
What life has in it to be lost;
And I could ask if what I saw,
Before me there, was man or ghost.

He may have died so many times
That all there was of him to see
Was pride, that kept itself alive
As too rebellious to be free;
He may have told, when more than once
Humility seemed imminent,
How many a lonely time in vain
The Second Coming came and went.

Whether he still defies or not
The failure of an angry task
That relegates him out of time
To chaos, I can only ask.
But as I knew him, so he was;
And somewhere among men to-day
Those old, unyielding eyes may flash,
And flinch—and look the other way.

The Mill

The miller's wife had waited long,
     The tea was cold, the fire was dead;
And there might yet be nothing wrong
     In how he went and what he said:
"There are no millers any more,"

Was all that she had heard him say;
And he had lingered at the door
So long that it seemed yesterday.

Sick with a fear that had no form
She knew that she was there at last;
And in the mill there was a warm
And mealy fragrance of the past.
What else there was would only seem
To say again what he had meant;
And what was hanging from a beam
Would not have heeded where she went.

And if she thought it followed her,
She may have reasoned in the dark
That one way of the few there were
Would hide her and would leave no mark:
Black water, smooth above the weir
Like starry velvet in the night,
Though ruffled once, would soon appear
The same as ever to the sight.

The Dark Hills

Dark hills at evening in the west,
Where sunset hovers like a sound
Of golden horns that sang to rest
Old bones of warriors under ground,
Far now from all the bannered ways
Where flash the legions of the sun,
You fade—as if the last of days
Were fading, and all wars were done.

The Three Taverns

When the brethren heard of us, they came to meet us as far as Appii
Forum, and The Three Taverns.

—*(Acts xxviii, 15)*

Herodion, Apelles, Amplias,
And Andronicus? Is it you I see—
At last? And is it you now that are gazing
As if in doubt of me? Was I not saying
That I should come to Rome? I did say that;
And I said furthermore that I should go
On westward, where the gateway of the world
Lets in the central sea. I did say that,
But I say only, now, that I am Paul—
A prisoner of the Law, and of the Lord
A voice made free. If there be time enough
To live, I may have more to tell you then
Of western matters. I go now to Rome,
Where Cæsar waits for me, and I shall wait,
And Cæsar knows how long. In Cæsarea
There was a legend of Agrippa saying
In a light way to Festus, having heard
My deposition, that I might be free,
Had I stayed free of Cæsar; but the word
Of God would have it as you see it is—
And here I am. The cup that I shall drink
Is mine to drink—the moment or the place
Not mine to say. If it be now in Rome,
Be it now in Rome; and if your faith exceed
The shadow cast of hope, say not of me
Too surely or too soon that years and shipwreck,
And all the many deserts I have crossed
That are not named or regioned, have undone

Beyond the brevities of our mortal healing
The part of me that is the least of me.
You see an older man than he who fell
Prone to the earth when he was nigh Damascus,
Where the great light came down; yet I am he
That fell, and he that saw, and he that heard.
And I am here, at last; and if at last
I give myself to make another crumb
For this pernicious feast of time and men—
Well, I have seen too much of time and men
To fear the ravening or the wrath of either.

Yes, it is Paul you see—the Saul of Tarsus
That was a fiery Jew, and had men slain
For saying Something was beyond the Law,
And in ourselves. I fed my suffering soul
Upon the Law till I went famishing,
Not knowing that I starved. How should I know,
More then than any, that the food I had—
What else it may have been—was not for me?
My fathers and their fathers and their fathers
Had found it good, and said there was no other,
And I was of the line. When Stephen fell,
Among the stones that crushed his life away,
There was no place alive that I could see
For such a man. Why should a man be given
To live beyond the Law? So I said then,
As men say now to me. How then do I
Persist in living? Is that what you ask?
If so, let my appearance be for you
No living answer; for Time writes of death
On men before they die, and what you see
Is not the man. The man that you see not—
The man within the man—is most alive;

Though hatred would have ended, long ago,
The bane of his activities. I have lived,
Because the faith within me that is life
Endures to live, and shall, till soon or late,
Death, like a friend unseen, shall say to me
My toil is over and my work begun.

How often, and how many a time again,
Have I said I should be with you in Rome!
He who is always coming never comes,
Or comes too late, you may have told yourselves;
And I may tell you now that after me,
Whether I stay for little or for long,
The wolves are coming. Have an eye for them,
And a more careful ear for their confusion
Than you need have much longer for the sound
Of what I tell you—should I live to say
More than I say to Cæsar. What I know
Is down for you to read in what is written;
And if I cloud a little with my own
Mortality the gleam that is immortal,
I do it only because I am I—
Being on earth and of it, in so far
As time flays yet the remnant. This you know;
And if I sting men, as I do sometimes,
With a sharp word that hurts, it is because
Man's habit is to feel before he sees;
And I am of a race that feels. Moreover,
The world is here for what is not yet here
For more than are a few; and even in Rome,
Where men are so enamored of the Cross
That fame has echoed, and increasingly,
The music of your love and of your faith
To foreign ears that are as far away

As Antioch and Haran, yet I wonder
How much of love you know, and if your faith
Be the shut fruit of words. If so, remember
Words are but shells unfilled. Jews have at least
A Law to make them sorry they were born
If they go long without it; and these Gentiles,
For the first time in shrieking history,
Have love and law together, if so they will,
For their defense and their immunity
In these last days. Rome, if I know the name,
Will have anon a crown of thorns and fire
Made ready for the wreathing of new masters,
Of whom we are appointed, you and I,—
And you are still to be when I am gone,
Should I go presently. Let the word fall,
Meanwhile, upon the dragon-ridden field
Of circumstance, either to live or die;
Concerning which there is a parable,
Made easy for the comfort and attention
Of those who preach, fearing they preach in vain.
You are to plant, and then to plant again
Where you have gathered, gathering as you go;
For you are in the fields that are eternal,
And you have not the burden of the Lord
Upon your mortal shoulders. What you have
Is a light yoke, made lighter by the wearing,
Till it shall have the wonder and the weight
Of a clear jewel, shining with a light
Wherein the sun and all the fiery stars
May soon be fading. When Gamaliel said
That if they be of men these things are nothing
But if they be of God, they are for none
To overthrow, he spoke as a good Jew,
And one who stayed a Jew; and he said all.

And you know, by the temper of your faith,
How far the fire is in you that I felt
Before I knew Damascus. A word here,
Or there, or not there, or not anywhere,
Is not the Word that lives and is the life;
And you, therefore, need weary not yourselves
With jealous aches of others. If the world
Were not a world of aches and innovations,
Attainment would have no more joy of it.
There will be creeds and schisms, creeds in creeds,
And schisms in schisms; myriads will be done
To death because a farthing has two sides,
And is at last a farthing. Telling you this,
I, who bid men to live, appeal to Cæsar.
Once I had said the ways of God were dark,
Meaning by that the dark ways of the Law.
Such is the Glory of our tribulations;
For the Law kills the flesh that kills the Law,
And we are then alive. We have eyes then;
And we have then the Cross between two worlds—
To guide us, or to blind us for a time,
Till we have eyes indeed. The fire that smites
A few on highways, changing all at once,
Is not for all. The power that holds the world
Away from God that holds himself away—
Farther away than all your works and words
Are like to fly without the wings of faith—
Was not, nor ever shall be, a small hazard
Enlivening the ways of easy leisure
Or the cold road of knowledge. When our eyes
Have wisdom, we see more than we remember;
And the old world of our captivities
May then become a smitten glimpse of ruin,
Like one where vanished hewers have had their day

Of wrath on Lebanon. Before we see,
Meanwhile, we suffer; and I come to you,
At last, through many storms and through much night.

Yet whatsoever I have undergone,
My keepers in this instance are not hard.
But for the chance of an ingratitude,
I might indeed be curious of their mercy,
And fearful of their leisure while I wait,
A few leagues out of Rome. Men go to Rome,
Not always to return—but not that now.
Meanwhile, I seem to think you look at me
With eyes that are at last more credulous
Of my identity. You remark in me
No sort of leaping giant, though some words
Of mine to you from Corinth may have leapt
A little through your eyes into your soul.
I trust they were alive, and are alive
Today; for there be none that shall indite
So much of nothing as the man of words
Who writes in the Lord's name for his name's sake
And has not in his blood the fire of time
To warm eternity. Let such a man—
If once the light is in him and endures—
Content himself to be the general man,
Set free to sift the decencies and thereby
To learn, except he be one set aside
For sorrow, more of pleasure than of pain;
Though if his light be not the light indeed,
But a brief shine that never really was,
And fails, leaving him worse than where he was,
Then shall he be of all men destitute.
And here were not an issue for much ink,
Or much offending faction among scribes.

The Kingdom is within us, we are told;
And when I say to you that we possess it
In such a measure as faith makes it ours,
I say it with a sinner's privilege
Of having seen and heard, and seen again,
After a darkness; and if I affirm
To the last hour that faith affords alone
The Kingdom entrance and an entertainment,
I do not see myself as one who says
To man that he shall sit with folded hands
Against the Coming. If I be anything,
I move a driven agent among my kind,
Establishing by the faith of Abraham,
And by the grace of their necessities,
The clamoring word that is the word of life
Nearer than heretofore to the solution
Of their tomb-serving doubts. If I have loosed
A shaft of language that has flown sometimes
A little higher than the hearts and heads
Of nature's minions, it will yet be heard,
Like a new song that waits for distant ears.
I cannot be the man that I am not;
And while I own that earth is my affliction,
I am a man of earth, who says not all
To all alike. That were impossible.
Even as it were so that He should plant
A larger garden first. But you today
Are for the larger sowing; and your seed,
A little mixed, will have, as He foresaw,
The foreign harvest of a wider growth,
And one without an end. Many there are,
And are to be, that shall partake of it,
Though none may share it with an understanding
That is not his alone. We are all alone;

And yet we are all parcelled of one order—
Jew, Gentile, or barbarian in the dark
Of wildernesses that are not so much
As names yet in a book. And there are many,
Finding at last that words are not the Word,
And finding only that, will flourish aloft,
Like heads of captured Pharisees on pikes,
Our contradictions and discrepancies;
And there are many more will hang themselves
Upon the letter, seeing not in the Word
The friend of all who fail, and in their faith
A sword of excellence to cut them down.

As long as there are glasses that are dark—
And there are many—we see darkly through them;
All which have I conceded and set down
In words that have no shadow. What is dark
Is dark, and we may not say otherwise;
Yet what may be as dark as a lost fire
For one of us, may still be for another
A coming gleam across the gulf of ages,
And a way home from shipwreck to the shore;
And so, through pangs and ills and desperations,
There may be light for all. There shall be light.
As much as that, you know. You cannot say
This woman or that man will be the next
On whom it falls; you are not here for that.
Your ministration is to be for others
The firing of a rush that may for them
Be soon the fire itself. The few at first
Are fighting for the multitude at last;
Therefore remember what Gamaliel said
Before you, when the sick were lying down
In streets all night for Peter's passing shadow.

Fight, and say what you feel; say more than words.
Give men to know that even their days of earth
To come are more than ages that are gone.
Say what you feel, while you have time to say it.
Eternity will answer for itself,
Without your intercession; yet the way
For many is a long one, and as dark,
Meanwhile, as dreams of hell. See not your toil
Too much, and if I be away from you
Think of me as a brother to yourselves,
Of many blemishes. Beware of stoics,
And give your left hand to grammarians;
And when you seem, as many a time you may,
To have no other friend than hope, remember
That you are not the first, or yet the last.

The best of life, until we see beyond
The shadows of ourselves (and they are less
Than even the blindest of indignant eyes
Would have them) is in what we do not know.
Make, then, for all your fears a place to sleep
With all your faded sins; nor think yourselves
Egregious and alone for your defects
Of youth and yesterday. I was young once;
And there's a question if you played the fool
With a more fervid and inherent zeal
Than I have in my story to remember,
Or gave your necks to folly's conquering foot,
Or flung yourselves with an unstudied aim,
More frequently than I. Never mind that.
Man's little house of days will hold enough,
Sometimes, to make him wish it were not his,
But it will not hold all. Things that are dead
Are best without it, and they own their death

By virtue of their dying. Let them go,—
But think you not the world is ashes yet,
And you have all the fire. The world is here
Today, and it may not be gone tomorrow;
For there are millions, and there may be more,
To make in turn a various estimation
Of its old ills and ashes, and the traps
Of its apparent wrath. Many with ears
That hear not yet, shall have ears given to them,
And then they shall hear strangely. Many with eyes
That are incredulous of the Mystery
Shall yet be driven to feel, and then to read
Where language has an end and is a veil,
Not woven of our words. Many that hate
Their kind are soon to know that without love
Their faith is but the perjured name of nothing.
I that have done some hating in my time
See now no time for hate; I that have left,
Fading behind me like familiar lights
That are to shine no more for my returning,
Home, friends, and honors,—I that have lost all else
For wisdom, and the wealth of it, say now
To you that out of wisdom has come love,
That measures and is of itself the measure
Of works and hope and faith. Your longest hours
Are not so long that you may torture them
And harass not yourselves; and the last days
Are on the way that you prepare for them,
And was prepared for you, here in a world
Where you have sinned and suffered, striven and seen.
If you be not so hot for counting them
Before they come that you consume yourselves,
Peace may attend you all in these last days—
And me, as well as you. Yes, even in Rome.

Well, I have talked and rested, though I fear
My rest has not been yours; in which event,
Forgive one who is only seven leagues
From Cæsar. When I told you I should come,
I did not see myself the criminal
You contemplate, for seeing beyond the Law
That which the Law saw not. But this, indeed,
Was good of you, and I shall not forget;
No, I shall not forget you came so far
To meet a man so dangerous. Well, farewell.
They come to tell me I am going now—
With them. I hope that we shall meet again,
But none may say what he shall find in Rome.

Tact

Observant of the way she told
        So much of what was true,
No vanity could long withhold
        Regard that was her due:
She spared him the familiar guile,
        So easily achieved,
That only made a man to smile
        And left him undeceived.

Aware that all imagining
        Of more than what she meant
Would urge an end of everything,
        He stayed; and when he went,
They parted with a merry word
        That was to him as light
As any that was ever heard
        Upon a starry night.

She smiled a little, knowing well
    That he would not remark
The ruins of a day that fell

    Around her in the dark:
He saw no ruins anywhere,
    Nor fancied there were scars
On anyone who lingered there,
    Alone below the stars.

Archibald's Example

Old Archibald, in his eternal chair,
Where trespassers, whatever their degree,
Were soon frowned out again, was looking off
Across the clover when he said to me:

"My green hill yonder, where the sun goes down
Without a scratch, was once inhabited
By trees that injured him—an evil trash
That made a cage, and held him while he bled.

"Gone fifty years, I see them as they were
Before they fell. They were a crooked lot
To spoil my sunset, and I saw no time
In fifty years for crooked things to rot.

"Trees, yes; but not a service or a joy
To God or man, for they were thieves of light.
So down they came. Nature and I looked on,
And we were glad when they were out of sight.

"Trees are like men, sometimes; and that being so,
So much for that." He twinkled in his chair,
And looked across the clover to the place
That he remembered when the trees were there.

Souvenir

A vanished house that for an hour I knew
By some forgotten chance when I was young
Had once a glimmering window overhung
With honeysuckle wet with evening dew.
Along the path tall dusky dahlias grew,
And shadowy hydrangeas reached and swung
Ferociously; and over me, among
The moths and mysteries, a blurred bat flew.

Somewhere within there were dim presences
Of days that hovered and of years gone by.
I waited, and between their silences
There was an evanescent faded noise;
And though a child, I knew it was the voice
Of one whose occupation was to die.

An Evangelist's Wife

"Why am I not myself these many days,
You ask? And have you nothing more to ask?
I do you wrong? I do not hear your praise
To God for giving you me to share your task?

"Jealous—of Her? Because her cheeks are pink,
And she has eyes? No, not if she had seven.
If you should only steal an hour to think,
Sometime, there might be less to be forgiven.

"No, you are never cruel. If once or twice
I found you so, I could applaud and sing.
Jealous of—What? You are not very wise.
Does not the good Book tell you anything?

"In David's time poor Michal had to go.
Jealous of God? Well, if you like it so."

Lazarus

"No, Mary, there was nothing—not a word.
Nothing, and always nothing. Go again
Yourself, and he may listen—or at least
Look up at you, and let you see his eyes.
I might as well have been the sound of rain,
A wind among the cedars, or a bird;
Or nothing. Mary, make him look at you;
And even if he should say that we are nothing,
To know that you have heard him will be something.
And yet he loved us, and it was for love
The Master gave him back. Why did he wait
So long before he came? Why did he weep?
I thought he would be glad—and Lazarus—
To see us all again as he had left us—
All as it was, all as it was before."

Mary, who felt her sister's frightened arms
Like those of someone drowning who had seized her,
Fearing at last they were to fail and sink
Together in this fog-stricken sea of strangeness,
Fought sadly, with bereaved indignant eyes,
To find again the fading shores of home
That she had seen but now could see no longer
Now she could only gaze into the twilight,
And in the dimness know that he was there,
Like someone that was not. He who had been
Their brother, and was dead, now seemed alive
Only in death again—or worse than death;
For tombs at least, always until today,
Though sad were certain. There was nothing certain
For man or God in such a day as this;
For there they were alone, and there was he—
Alone; and somewhere out of Bethany,
The Master—who had come to them so late,
Only for love of them and then so slowly,
And was for their sake hunted now by men
Who feared Him as they feared no other prey—
For the world's sake was hidden. "Better the tomb
For Lazarus than life, if this be life,"
She thought; and then to Martha, "No, my dear,"
She said aloud; "not as it was before.
Nothing is ever as it was before,
Where Time has been. Here there is more than Time;
And we that are so lonely and so far
From home, since he is with us here again,
Are farther now from him and from ourselves
Than we are from the stars. He will not speak
Until the spirit that is in him speaks;
And we must wait for all we are to know,
Or even to learn that we are not to know.

Martha, we are too near to this for knowledge,
And that is why it is that we must wait.
Our friends are coming if we call for them,
And there are covers we'll put over him
To make him warmer. We are too young, perhaps,
To say that we know better what is best
Than he. We do not know how old he is.
If you remember what the Master said,
Try to believe that we need have no fear.
Let me, the selfish and the careless one,
Be housewife and a mother for tonight;
For I am not so fearful as you are,
And I was not so eager."

                Martha sank
Down at her sister's feet and there sat watching
A flower that had a small familiar name
That was as old as memory, but was not
The name of what she saw now in its brief
And infinite mystery that so frightened her
That life became a terror. Tears again
Flooded her eyes and overflowed. "No, Mary,"
She murmured slowly, hating her own words
Before she heard them, "you are not so eager
To see our brother as we see him now;
Neither is he who gave him back to us.
I was to be the simple one, as always,
And this was all for me." She stared again
Over among the trees where Lazarus,
Who seemed to be a man who was not there,
Might have been one more shadow among shadows,
·If she had not remembered. Then she felt
The cool calm hands of Mary on her face,
And shivered, wondering if such hands were real.

"The Master loved you as he loved us all,
Martha; and you are saying only things
That children say when they have had no sleep.
Try somehow now to rest a little while;
You know that I am here, and that our friends
Are coming if I call."

                                    Martha at last
Arose, and went with Mary to the door,
Where they stood looking off at the same place,
And at the same shape that was always there
As if it would not ever move or speak,
And always would be there. "Mary, go now,
Before the dark that will be coming hides him.
I am afraid of him out there alone,
Unless I see him; and I have forgotten
What sleep is. Go now—make him look at you—
And I shall hear him if he stirs or whispers.
Go!—or I'll scream and bring all Bethany
To come and make him speak. Make him say once
That he is glad, and God may say the rest.
Though He say I shall sleep, and sleep for ever,
I shall not care for that . . . Go!"

                                    Mary, moving
Almost as if an angry child had pushed her,
Went forward a few steps; and having waited
As long as Martha's eyes would look at hers,
Went forward a few more, and a few more;
And so, until she came to Lazarus,
Who crouched with his face hidden in his hands,
Like one that had no face. Before she spoke,
Feeling her sister's eyes that were behind her
As if the door where Martha stood were now

As far from her as Egypt, Mary turned
Once more to see that she was there. Then, softly,
Fearing him not so much as wondering
What his first word might be, said, "Lazarus,
Forgive us if we seemed afraid of you;"
And having spoken, pitied her poor speech
That had so little seeming gladness in it,
So little comfort, and so little love.

There was no sign from him that he had heard,
Or that he knew that she was there, or cared
Whether she spoke to him again or died
There at his feet. "We love you, Lazarus,
And we are not afraid. The Master said
We need not be afraid. Will you not say
To me that you are glad? Look, Lazarus!
Look at my face, and see me. This is Mary."
She found his hands and held them. They were cool,
Like hers, but they were not so calm as hers.
Through the white robes in which his friends had wrapped
        him
When he had groped out of that awful sleep,
She felt him trembling and she was afraid.
At last he sighed; and she prayed hungrily
To God that she might hear again the voice
Of Lazarus, whose hands were giving her now
The recognition of a living pressure
That was almost a language. When he spoke,
Only one word that she had waited for
Came from his lips, and that word was her name.

"I heard them saying, Mary, that he wept
Before I woke." The words were low and shaken,
Yet Mary knew that he who uttered them

Was Lazarus; and that would be enough
Until there should be more . . . "Who made him come,
That he should weep for me? . . . Was it you, Mary?"
The questions held in his incredulous eyes
Were more than she would see. She looked away;
But she had felt them and should feel for ever,
She thought, their cold and lonely desperation
That had the bitterness of all cold things
That were not cruel. "I should have wept," he said,
"If I had been the Master. . . ."

                              Now she could feel
His hands above her hair—the same black hair
That once he made a jest of, praising it,
While Martha's busy eyes had left their work
To flash with laughing envy. Nothing of that
Was to be theirs again; and such a thought
Was like the flying by of a quick bird
Seen through a shadowy doorway in the twilight.
For now she felt his hands upon her head,
Like weights of kindness: "I forgive you, Mary. . . .
You did not know—Martha could not have known—
Only the Master knew. . . . Where is he now?
Yes, I remember. They came after him.
May the good God forgive him. . . . I forgive him.
I must; and I may know only from him
The burden of all this . . . Martha was here—
But I was not yet here. She was afraid. . . .
Why did he do it, Mary? Was it—you?
Was it for you? . . . Where are the friends I saw?
Yes, I remember. They all went away.
I made them go away. . . . Where is he now? . . .
What do I see down there? Do I see Martha—
Down by the door? . . . I must have time for this."

Lazarus looked about him fearfully,
And then again at Mary, who discovered
Awakening apprehension in his eyes,
And shivered at his feet. All she had feared
Was here; and only in the slow reproach
Of his forgiveness lived his gratitude.
Why had he asked if it was all for her
That he was here? And what had Martha meant?
Why had the Master waited? What was coming
To Lazarus, and to them, that had not come?
What had the Master seen before he came,
That he had come so late?

                  "Where is he, Mary?"
Lazarus asked again. "Where did he go?"
Once more he gazed about him, and once more
At Mary for an answer. "Have they found him?
Or did he go away because he wished
Never to look into my eyes again? . . .
That, I could understand. . . . Where is he, Mary?"

"I do not know," she said. "Yet in my heart
I know that he is living, as you are living—
Living, and here. He is not far from us.
He will come back to us and find us all—
Lazarus, Martha, Mary—everything—
All as it was before. Martha said that.
And he said we were not to be afraid."
Lazarus closed his eyes while on his face
A tortured adumbration of a smile
Flickered an instant. "All as it was before,"
He murmured wearily. "Martha said that;
And he said you were not to be afraid . . .
Not you . . . Not you . . . Why should you be afraid?

Give all your little fears, and Martha's with them,
To me; and I will add them unto mine,
Like a few rain-drops to Gennesaret."

"If you had frightened me in other ways,
Not willing it," Mary said, "I should have known
You still for Lazarus. But who is this?
Tell me again that you are Lazarus;
And tell me if the Master gave to you
No sign of a new joy that shall be coming
To this house that he loved. Are you afraid?
Are you afraid, who have felt everything—
And seen . . . ?"

                    But Lazarus only shook his head,
Staring with his bewildered shining eyes
Hard into Mary's face. "I do not know,
Mary," he said, and after a long time,
"When I came back, I knew the Master's eyes
Were looking into mine. I looked at his,
And there was more in them than I could see.
At first I could see nothing but his eyes;
Nothing else anywhere was to be seen—
Only his eyes. And they looked into mine—
Long into mine, Mary, as if he knew."

Mary began to be afraid of words
As she had never been afraid before
Of loneliness or darkness, or of death,
But now she must have more of them or die:
"He cannot know that there is worse than death,"
She said. "And you . . . ."

                    "Yes, there is worse than death,"
Said Lazarus; "and that was what he knew;
And that is what it was that I could see
This morning in his eyes. I was afraid,
But not as you are. There is worse than death,
Mary; and there is nothing that is good
For you in dying while you are still here.
Mary, never go back to that again.
You would not hear me if I told you more,
For I should say it only in a language
That you are not to learn by going back.
To be a child again is to go forward—
And that is much to know. Many grow old,
And fade, and go away, not knowing how much
That is to know. Mary, the night is coming,
And there will soon be darkness all around you.
Let us go down where Martha waits for us,
And let there be light shining in this house."

He rose, but Mary would not let him go:
"Martha, when she came back from here, said only
That she heard nothing. And have you no more
For Mary now than you had then for Martha?
Is Nothing, Lazarus, all you have for me?
Was Nothing all you found where you have been?
If that be so, what is there worse than that—
Or better—if that be so? And why should you,
With even our love, go the same dark road over?"

"I could not answer that, if that were so,"
Said Lazarus,—"not even if I were God.
Why should He care whether I came or stayed,
If that were so? Why should the Master weep—
For me, or for the world,—or save himself

Longer for nothing? And if that were so,
Why should a few years' more mortality
Make him a fugitive where flight were needless,
Had he but held his peace and given his nod
To an old Law that would be new as any?
I cannot say the answer to all that;
Though I may say that he is not afraid,
And that it is not for the joy there is
In serving an eternal Ignorance
Of our futility that he is here.
Is that what you and Martha mean by Nothing?
Is that what you are fearing? If that be so,
There are more weeds than lentils in your garden.
And one whose weeds are laughing at his harvest
May as well have no garden; for not there
Shall he be gleaning the few bits and orts
Of life that are to save him. For my part,
I am again with you, here among shadows
That will not always be so dark as this;
Though now I see there's yet an evil in me
That made me let you be afraid of me.
No, I was not afraid—not even of life.
I thought I was . . . I must have time for this;
And all the time there is will not be long.
I cannot tell you what the Master saw
This morning in my eyes. I do not know.
I cannot yet say how far I have gone,
Or why it is that I am here again,
Or where the old road leads. I do not know.
I know that when I did come back, I saw
His eyes again among the trees and faces—
Only his eyes; and they looked into mine—
Long into mine—long, long, as if he knew."

Mr. Flood's Party

Old Eben Flood, climbing alone one night
Over the hill between the two below
And the forsaken upland hermitage
That held as much as he should ever know
On earth again of home, paused warily.
The road was his with not a native near;
And Eben, having leisure, said aloud,
For no man else in Tilbury Town to hear:

"Well, Mr. Flood, we have the harvest moon
Again, and we may not have many more;
The bird is on the wing, the poet says,
And you and I have said it here before.
Drink to the bird." He raised up to the light
The jug that he had gone so far to fill,
And answered huskily: "Well, Mr. Flood,
Since you propose it, I believe I will."

Alone, as if enduring to the end
A valiant armor of scarred hopes outworn,
He stood there in the middle of the road
Like Roland's ghost winding a silent horn.
Below him, in the town among the trees,
Where friends of others days had honored him,
A phantom salutation of the dead
Rang thinly till old Eben's eyes were dim.

Then, as a mother lays her sleeping child
Down tenderly, fearing it may awake,
He set the jug down slowly at his feet
With trembling care, knowing that most things break;
And only when assured that on firm earth

It stood, as the uncertain lives of men
Assuredly did not, he paced away,
And with his hand extended paused again:

"Well, Mr. Flood, we have not met like this
In a long time; and many a change has come
To both of us, I fear, since last it was
We had a drop together. Welcome home!"
Convivially returning with himself,
Again he raised the jug up to the light;
And with an acquiescent quaver said:
"Well, Mr. Flood, if you insist, I might.

"Only a very little, Mr. Flood—
For auld lang syne. No more, sir; that will do."
So, for the time, apparently it did,
And Eben evidently thought so too;
For soon amid the silver loneliness
Of night he lifted up his voice and sang,
Secure, with only two moons listening,
Until the whole harmonious landscape rang—

"For auld lang syne." The weary throat gave out,
The last word wavered, and the song was done.
He raised again the jug regretfully
And shook his head, and was again alone.
There was not much that was ahead of him,
And there was nothing in the town below—
Where strangers would have shut the many doors
That many friends had opened long ago.

Ben Trovato

The deacon thought. "I know them," he began,
"And they are all you ever heard of them—
Allurable to no sure theorem,
The scorn or the humility of man.
You say 'Can I believe it?'—and I can;
And I'm unwilling even to condemn
The benefaction of a stratagem
Like hers—and I'm a Presbyterian.

"Though blind, with but a wandering hour to live,
He felt the other woman in the fur
That now the wife had on. Could she forgive
All that? Apparently. Her rings were gone,
Of course; and when he found that she had none,
He smiled—as he had never smiled at her."

The Tree in Pamela's Garden

Pamela was too gentle to deceive
Her roses. "Let the men stay where they are,"
She said, "and if Apollo's avatar
Be one of them, I shall not have to grieve."
And so she made all Tilbury Town believe
She sighed a little more for the North Star
Than over men, and only in so far
As she was in a garden was like Eve.

Her neighbors—doing all that neighbors can
To make romance of reticence meanwhile—
Seeing that she had never loved a man,

Wished Pamela had a cat, or a small bird,
And only would have wondered at her smile
Could they have seen that she had overheard.

Vain Gratuities

Never was there a man much uglier
In eyes of other women, or more grim:
"The Lord has filled her chalice to the brim,
So let us pray she's a philosopher,"
They said; and there was more they said of her—
Deeming it, after twenty years with him,
No wonder that she kept her figure slim
And always made you think of lavender.

But she, demure as ever, and as fair,
Almost, as they remembered her before
She found him, would have laughed had she been there;
And all they said would have been heard no more
Than foam that washes on an island shore
Where there are none to listen or to care.

Lost Anchors

Like a dry fish flung inland far from shore,
There lived a sailor, warped and ocean-browned,
Who told of an old vessel, harbor-drowned
And out of mind a century before,
Where divers, on descending to explore
A legend that had lived its way around
The world of ships, in the dark hulk had found
Anchors, which had been seized and seen no more.

Improving a dry leisure to invest
Their misadventure with a manifest
Analogy that he may read who runs,
The sailor made it old as ocean grass—
Telling of much that once had come to pass
With him, whose mother should have had no sons.

Recalled

Long after there were none of them alive
About the place—where there is now no place
But a walled hole where fruitless vines embrace
Their parent skeletons that yet survive
In evil thorns—none of us could arrive
At a more cogent answer to their ways
Than one old Isaac in his latter days
Had humor or compassion to contrive.

I mentioned them, and Isaac shook his head:
"The Power that you call yours and I call mine
Extinguished in the last of them a line
That Satan would have disinherited.
When we are done with all but the Divine,
We die." And there was no more to be said.

Caput Mortuum

Not even if with a wizard force I might
Have summoned whomsoever I would name,
Should anyone else have come than he who came,
Uncalled, to share with me my fire that night;
For though I should have said that all was right,

Or right enough, nothing had been the same
As when I found him there before the flame,
Always a welcome and a useful sight.

Unfailing and exuberant all the time,
Having no gold he paid with golden rhyme,
Of older coinage than his old defeat,
A debt that like himself was obsolete
In Art's long hazard, where no man may choose
Whether he play to win or toil to lose.

The Long Race

Up the old hill to the old house again
Where fifty years ago the friend was young
Who should be waiting somewhere there among
Old things that least remembered most remain,
He toiled on with a pleasure that was pain
To think how soon asunder would be flung
The curtain half a century had hung
Between the two ambitions they had slain.

They dredged an hour for words, and then were done.
"Good-bye!... You have the same old weather-vane—
Your little horse that's always on the run."
And all the way down back to the next train,
Down the old hill to the old road again,
It seemed as if the little horse had won.

Many Are Called

The Lord Apollo, who has never died,
Still holds alone his immemorial reign,
Supreme in an impregnable domain
That with his magic he has fortified;
And though melodious multitudes have tried
In ecstasy, in anguish, and in vain,
With invocation sacred and profane
To lure him, even the loudest are outside.

Only at unconjectured intervals,
By will of him on whom no man may gaze,
By word of him whose law no man has read,
A questing light may rift the sullen walls,
To cling where mostly its infrequent rays
Fall golden on the patience of the dead.

Rembrandt to Rembrandt

(Amsterdam, 1645)

And there you are again, now as you are.
Observe yourself as you discern yourself
In your discredited ascendency;
Without your velvet or your feathers now,
Commend your new condition to your fate,
And your conviction to the sieves of time.
Meanwhile appraise yourself, Rembrandt van Ryn,
Now as you are—formerly more or less
Distinguished in the civil scenery,
And once a painter. There you are again,
Where you may see that you have on your shoulders

No lovelier burden for an ornament
Than one man's head that's yours. Praise be to God
That you have that; for you are like enough
To need it now, my friend, and from now on;
For there are shadows and obscurities
Immediate or impending on your view,
That may be worse than you have ever painted
For the bewildered and unhappy scorn
Of injured Hollanders in Amsterdam
Who cannot find their fifty florins' worth
Of Holland face where you have hidden it
In your new golden shadow that excites them,
Or see that when the Lord made color and light
He made not one thing only, or believe
That shadows are not nothing. Saskia said,
Before she died, how they would swear at you,
And in commiseration at themselves.
She laughed a little, too, to think of them—
And then at me. . . . That was before she died.

And I could wonder, as I look at you,
There as I have you now, there as you are,
Or nearly so as any skill of mine
Has ever caught you in a bilious mirror,—
Yes, I could wonder long, and with a reason,
If all but everything achievable
In me were not achieved and lost already,
Like a fool's gold. But you there in the glass,
And you there on the canvas, have a sort
Of solemn doubt about it; and that's well
For Rembrandt and for Titus. All that's left
Of all that was is here; and all that's here
Is one man who remembers, and one child
Beginning to forget. One, two, and three,

The others died, and then—then Saskia died;
And then, so men believe, the painter died.
So men believe. So it all comes at once.
And here's a fellow painting in the dark,—
A loon who cannot see that he is dead
Before God lets him die. He paints away
At the impossible, so Holland has it,
For venom or for spite, or for defection,
Or else for God knows what. Well, if God knows,
And Rembrandt knows, it matters not so much
What Holland knows or cares. If Holland wants
Its heads all in a row, and all alike,
There's Franz to do them and to do them well—
Rat-catchers, archers, or apothecaries,
And one as like a rabbit as another.
Value received, and every Dutchman happy.
All's one to Franz, and to the rest of them,—
Their ways being theirs, are theirs.—But you, my friend,
If I have made you something as you are,
Will need those jaws and eyes and all the fight
And fire that's in them, and a little more,
To take you on and the world after you;
For now you fare alone, without the fashion
To sing you back and fling a flower or two
At your accusing feet. Poor Saskia saw
This coming that has come, and with a guile
Of kindliness that covered half her doubts
Would give me gold, and laugh... before she died.

And if I see the road that you are going,
You that are not so jaunty as aforetime,
God knows if she were not appointed well
To die. She might have wearied of it all
Before the worst was over, or begun.

A woman waiting on a man's avouch
Of the invisible, may not wait always
Without a word betweenwhiles, or a dash
Of poison on his faith. Yes, even she.
She might have come to see at last with others,
And then to say with others, who say more,
That you are groping on a phantom trail
Determining a dusky way to nowhere;
That errors unconfessed and obstinate
Have teemed and cankered in you for so long
That even your eyes are sick, and you see light
Only because you dare not see the dark
That is around you and ahead of you.
She might have come, by ruinous estimation
Of old applause and outworn vanities,
To clothe you over in a shroud of dreams,
And so be nearer to the counterfeit
Of her invention than aware of yours.
She might, as well as any, by this time,
Unwillingly and eagerly have bitten
Another devil's-apple of unrest,
And so, by some attendant artifice
Or other, might anon have had you sharing
A taste that would have tainted everything,
And so had been for two, instead of one,
The taste of death in life—which is the food
Of art that has betrayed itself alive
And is a food of hell. She might have heard
Unhappily the temporary noise
Of louder names than yours, and on frail urns
That hardly will ensure a dwelling-place
For even the dust that may be left of them,
She might, and angrily, as like as not,
Look soon to find your name, not finding it.

She might, like many another born for joy
And for sufficient fulness of the hour,
Go famishing by now, and in the eyes
Of pitying friends and dwindling satellites
Be told of no uncertain dereliction
Touching the cold offence of my decline.
And even if this were so, and she were here
Again to make a fact of all my fancy,
How should I ask of her to see with me
Through night where many a time I seem in vain
To seek for new assurance of a gleam
That comes at last, and then, so it appears,
Only for you and me—and a few more,
Perchance, albeit their faces are not many
Among the ruins that are now around us.
That was a fall, my friend, we had together—
Or rather it was my house, mine alone,
That fell, leaving you safe. Be glad for that.
There's life in you that shall outlive my clay
That's for a time alive and will in time
Be nothing—but not yet. You that are there
Where I have painted you are safe enough,
Though I see dragons. Verily, that was a fall—
A dislocating fall, a blinding fall,
A fall indeed. But there are no bones broken;
And even the teeth and eyes that I make out
Among the shadows, intermittently,
Show not so firm in their accoutrement
Of terror-laden unreality
As you in your neglect of their performance,—
Though for their season we must humor them
For what they are: devils undoubtedly,
But not so perilous and implacable
In their undoing of poor human triumph

As easy fashion—or brief novelty
That ails even while it grows, and like sick fruit
Falls down anon to an indifferent earth
To break with inward rot. I say all this,
And I concede, in honor of your silence,
A waste of innocent facility
In tints of other colors than are mine.
I cannot paint with words, but there's a time
For most of us when words are all we have
To serve our stricken souls. And here you say,
"Be careful, or you may commit your soul
Soon to the very devil of your denial."
I might have wagered on you to say that,
Knowing that I believe in you too surely
To spoil you with a kick or paint you over.

No, my good friend, Mynheer Rembrandt van Ryn—
Sometime a personage in Amsterdam,
But now not much—I shall not give myself
To be the sport of any dragon-spawn
Of Holland, or elsewhere. Holland was hell
Not long ago, and there were dragons then
More to be fought than any of these we see
That we may foster now. They are not real,
But not for that the less to be regarded;
For there are slimy tyrants born of nothing
That harden slowly into seeming life
And have the strength of madness. I confess,
Accordingly, the wisdom of your care
That I look out for them. Whether I would
Or not, I must; and here we are as one
With our necessity. For though you loom
A little harsh in your respect of time
And circumstance, and of ordained eclipse,

We know together of a golden flood
That with its overflow shall drown away
The dikes that held it; and we know thereby
That in its rising light there lives a fire
No devils that are lodging here in Holland
Shall put out wholly, or much agitate,
Except in unofficial preparation
They put out first the sun. It's well enough
To think of them; wherefore I thank you, sir,
Alike for your remembrance and attention.

But there are demons that are longer-lived
Than doubts that have a brief and evil term
To congregate among the futile shards
And architraves of eminent collapse.
They are a many-favored family,
All told, with not a misbegotten dwarf
Among the rest that I can love so little
As one occult abortion in especial
Who perches on a picture (when it's done)
And says, "What of it, Rembrandt, if you do?"
This incubus would seem to be a sort
Of chorus, indicating, for our good,
The silence of the few friends that are left:
"What of it, Rembrandt, even if you know?"
It says again; "and you don't know for certain.
What if in fifty or a hundred years
They find you out? You may have gone meanwhile
So greatly to the dogs that you'll not care
Much what they find. If this be all you are—
This unaccountable aspiring insect—
You'll sleep as easy in oblivion
As any sacred monk or parricide;
And if, as you conceive, you are eternal,

Your soul may laugh, remembering (if a soul
Remembers) your befrenzied aspiration
To smear with certain ochres and some oil
A few more perishable ells of cloth,
And once or twice, to square your vanity,
Prove it was you alone that should achieve
A mortal eye—that may, no less, tomorrow
Show an immortal reason why today
Men see no more. And what's a mortal eye
More than a mortal herring, who has eyes
As well as you? Why not paint herrings, Rembrandt?
Or if not herrings, why not a split beef?
Perceive it only in its unalloyed
Integrity, and you may find in it
A beautified accomplishment no less
Indigenous than one that appertains
To gentlemen and ladies eating it.
The same God planned and made you, beef and human;
And one, but for His whim, might be the other."

That's how he says it, Rembrandt, if you listen;
He says it, and he goes. And then, sometimes,
There comes another spirit in his place—
One with a more engaging argument,
And with a softer note for saying truth
Not soft. Whether it be the truth or not,
I name it so; for there's a string in me
Somewhere that answers—which is natural,
Since I am but a living instrument
Played on by powers that are invisible.
"You might go faster, if not quite so far,"
He says, "if in your vexed economy
There lived a faculty for saying yes
And meaning no, and then for doing neither;

But since Apollo sees it otherwise,
Your Dutchmen, who are swearing at you still
For your pernicious filching of their florins,
May likely curse you down their generation,
Not having understood there was no malice
Or grinning evil in a golden shadow
That shall outshine their slight identities
And hold their faces when their names are nothing.
But this, as you discern, or should by now
Surmise, for you is neither here nor there:
You made your picture as your demon willed it;
That's about all of that. Now make as many
As may be to be made,—for so you will,
Whatever the toll may be, and hold your light
So that you see, without so much to blind you
As even the cobweb-flash of a misgiving,
Assured and certain that if you see right
Others will have to see—albeit their seeing
Shall irk them out of their serenity
For such a time as umbrage may require.
But there are many reptiles in the night
That now is coming on, and they are hungry;
And there's a Rembrandt to be satisfied
Who never will be, howsoever much
He be assured of an ascendency
That has not yet a shadow's worth of sound
Where Holland has its ears. And what of that?
Have you the weary leisure or sick wit
That breeds of its indifference a false envy
That is the vermin on accomplishment?
Are you inaugurating your new service
With fasting for a food you would not eat?
You are the servant, Rembrandt, not the master,—
But you are not assigned with other slaves

That in their freedom are the most in fear.
One of the few that are so fortunate
As to be told their task and to be given
A skill to do it with a tool too keen
For timid safety, bow your elected head
Under the stars tonight, and whip your devils
Each to his nest in hell. Forget your days,
And so forgive the years that may not be
So many as to be more than you may need
For your particular consistency
In your peculiar folly. You are counting
Some fewer years than forty at your heels;
And they have not pursued your gait so fast
As your oblivion—which has beaten them,
And rides now on your neck like an old man
With iron shins and fingers. Let him ride
(You haven't so much to say now about that),
And in a proper season let him run.
You may be dead then, even as you may now
Anticipate some other mortal strokes
Attending your felicity; and for that,
Oblivion heretofore has done some running
Away from graves, and will do more of it."

That's how it is your wiser spirit speaks,
Rembrandt. If you believe him, why complain?
If not, why paint? And why, in any event,
Look back for the old joy and the old roses,
Or the old fame? They are all gone together,
And Saskia with them; and with her left out,
They would avail no more now than one strand
Of Samson's hair wound round his little finger
Before the temple fell. Nor more are you
In any sudden danger to forget

That in Apollo's house there are no clocks
Or calendars to say for you in time
How far you are away from Amsterdam,
Or that the one same law that bids you see
Where now you see alone forbids in turn
Your light from Holland eyes till Holland ears
Are told of it; for that way, my good fellow,
Is one way more to death. If at the first
Of your long turning, which may still be longer
Than even your faith has measured it, you sigh
For distant welcome that may not be seen,
Or wayside shouting that will not be heard,
You may as well accommodate your greatness
To the convenience of an easy ditch,
And, anchored there with all your widowed gold,
Forget your darkness in the dark, and hear
No longer the cold wash of Holland scorn.

from *Tristram (the conclusion)*

            Isolt of the white hands,
Isolt with her gray eyes and her white face,
Still gazed across the water to the north
But not now for a ship. Were ships to come,
No fleet of them could hold a golden cargo
That would be worth one agate that was hers—
One toy that he had given her long ago,
And long ago forgotten. Yet there she gazed
Across the water, over the white waves,
Upon a castle that she had never seen,
And would not see, save as a phantom shape
Against a phantom sky. He had been there,
She thought, but not with her. He had died there,

But not for her. He had not thought of her,
Perhaps, and that was strange. He had been all,
And would be always all there was for her,
And he had not come back to her alive,
Not even to go again. It was like that
For women, sometimes, and might be so too often
For women like her. She hoped there were not many
Of them, or many of them to be, not knowing
More about that than about waves and foam,
And white birds everywhere, flying, and flying;
Alone, with her white face and her gray eyes,
She watched them there till even her thoughts were white,
And there was nothing alive but white birds flying,
Flying, and always flying, and still flying,
And the white sunlight flashing on the sea.

Haunted House

Here was a place where none would ever come
For shelter, save as we did from the rain.
We saw no ghost, yet once outside again
Each wondered why the other should be dumb;
For we had fronted nothing worse than gloom
And ruin, and to our vision it was plain
Where thrift, outshivering fear, had let remain
Some chairs that were like skeletons of home.

There were no trackless footsteps on the floor
Above us, and there were no sounds elsewhere.
But there was more than sound; and there was more
Than just an axe that once was in the air
Between us and the chimney, long before
Our time. So townsmen said who found her there.

The Sheaves

Where long the shadows of the wind had rolled,
Green wheat was yielding to the change assigned;
And as by some vast magic undivined
The world was turning slowly into gold.
Like nothing that ever bought or sold
It waited there, the body and the mind;
And with a mighty meaning of a kind
That tells the more the more it is not told.

So in a land where all days are not fair,
Fair days went on till on another day
A thousand golden sheaves were lying there,
Shining and still, but not for long to stay—
As if a thousand girls with golden hair
Might rise from where they slept and go away.

Karma

Christmas was in the air and all was well
With him, but for a few confusing flaws
In divers of God's images. Because
A friend of his would neither buy nor sell,
Was he to answer for the axe that fell?
He pondered; and the reason for it was,
Partly, a slowly freezing Santa Claus
Upon the corner, with his beard and bell.

Acknowledging an improvident surprise,
He magnified a fancy that he wished
The friend whom he had wrecked were here again.

Not sure of that, he found a compromise;
And from the fulness of his heart he fished
A dime for Jesus who had died for men.

New England

Here where the wind is always north-north-east
And children learn to walk on frozen toes,
Wonder begets an envy of all those
Who boil elsewhere with such a lyric yeast
Of love that you will hear them at a feast
Where demons would appeal for some repose,
Still clamoring where the chalice overflows
And crying wildest who have drunk the least.

Passion is here a soilure of the wits,
We're told, and Love a cross for them to bear;
Joy shivers in the corner where she knits
And Conscience always has the rocking-chair,
Cheerful as when she tortured into fits
The first cat that was ever killed by Care.

Reunion

By some derision of wild circumstance
Not then our pleasure somehow to perceive,
Last night we fell together to achieve
A light eclipse of years. But the pale chance
Of youth resumed was lost. Time gave a glance
At each of us, and there was no reprieve;
And when there was at last a way to leave,
Farewell was a foreseen extravagance.

Tonight the west has yet a failing red,
While silence whispers of all things not here;
And round there where the fire was that is dead,
Dusk-hidden tenants that are chairs appear.
The same old stars will soon be overhead,
But not so friendly and not quite so near.

Hector Kane

If Hector Kane at eighty-five
Was not the youngest man alive,
Appearance had anointed him
    With undiminished youth.
To look at him was to believe
That as we ask we may receive,
Annoyed by no such evil whim
    As death, or time, or truth.

Which is to doubt, if any of you,
Seeing him, had believed him true.
He was too young to be so old,
    Too old to be so fair.
Beneath a snowy crown of curls,
His cheeks that might have been a girl's
Were certainly, if truth were told,
    Too rose-like to be there.

But Hector was a child of earth,
And would have held of little worth
Reflection or misgiving cast
    On his reality.
It was a melancholy crime,

No less, to torture life with time;
And whoso did was first and last
    Creation's enemy.

He told us, one convivial night,
When younger men were not so bright
Or brisk as he, how he had spared
    His heart a world of pain,
Merely by seeing always clear
What most it was he wanted here,
And having it when most he cared,
    And having it again.

"You children of threescore or so,"
He said, "had best begin to know
If your infirmities that ache,
    Your lethargies and fears,
And doubts, are mostly more or less
Like things a drunkard in distress
May count with horror, while you shake
    For counting days and years.

"Nothing was ever true for me
Until I found it so," said he;
"So time for me has always been
    Four letters of a word.
Time? Is it anything to eat?
Or maybe it has legs and feet,
To go so as to be unseen;
    Or maybe it's a bird.

"Years? I have never seen such things.
Why let your fancy give them wings
To lift you from experience

And carry you astray?
If only you will not be old,
Your mines will give you more than gold,
And for a cheerful diligence
    Will keep the worm away.

"We die of what we eat and drink,
But more we die of what we think;
For which you see me still as young
    At heart as heretofore.
So here's to what's awaiting us—
Cras ingens iterabimus—"
A clutch of wonder gripped his tongue,
    And Hector said no more.

Serene and inarticulate
He lay, for us to contemplate.
The mortal trick, we all agreed,
    Was never better turned:
Bequeathing us to time and care,
He told us yet that we were there
To make as much as we could read
    Of all that he had learned.

About the Editor

Donald Hall is widely renowned as a poet. He is the author of thirteen books of verse, eighteen books of prose, and four books for children, and is also the editor of several anthologies and reference books. His most recent book of poetry is *The Museum of Clear Ideas*. He lives in New Hampshire.